ART
EXPRESS
BOOK 3

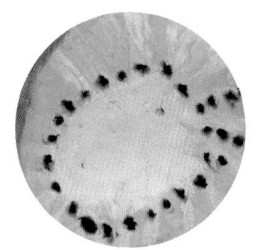

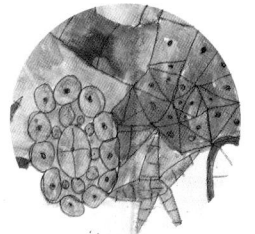

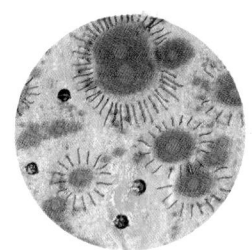

EILEEN ADAMS

ROSEMARY BIGNELL

JANE BOWER

JUDY GRAHAME

MICHÈLE CLAIRE KITTO

KEVIN MATHIESON

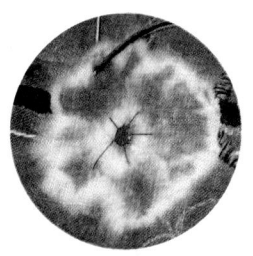

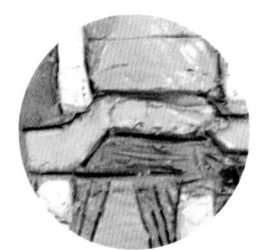

First published 2009
By A&C Black Publishers Ltd
36 Soho Square, London W1D 3QY
© 2009 A&C Black Publishers Ltd
ISBN 978 0 7136 8482 7 (Book & CD-ROM)
ISBN 978 1 4081 2220 4 (Site licence)

Unit text, and photographs unless otherwise stated © Eileen Adams (drawing); Rosemary Bignell (sculpture); Jane Bower (printing); Judy Grahame (painting); Michèle Claire Kitto (collage & textiles); Kevin Mathieson (digital technology)

CREDITS

Series Editor: *Julia Stanton*
Series Designer: *Elizabeth Healey*
Resource Sheet Designer: *Christina Newman*
   (Black Dog Design)
Editors: *Tanya Solomons, Monica Byles*
Picture Researchers: *Holly Beaumont,*
   Rebecca Barley
Illustrations: *Celia Hart*
CD-ROM Programming: *Q&D Ltd*
Publisher: *Linda Lambert*

ACKNOWLEDGEMENTS

The publishers would like to thank the following teachers who reviewed the material in their schools: Katie Epps and Laurence Keel. Also, the Editorial Board for their support during the project: Dan China, Jane Bower and Judy Grahame. The authors would like to thank the following schools for their help in facilitating the photographs used in the book.

Drawing: Thanks to Lynne Bebb, Carolyn Davies, Steven Follen; The Campaign for Drawing; Brookfield Primary School, Derby; Eveline Lowe Primary School, Southwark, London; Gillespie Primary School, Islington, London; Mount Stuart Primary School, Cardiff, Wales; Offmore First School, Kidderminster, Worcs.; Parsonage Farm Primary School, Rainham, Essex; Robinsfield Infant School, Westminster, London; Tollgate Primary School,

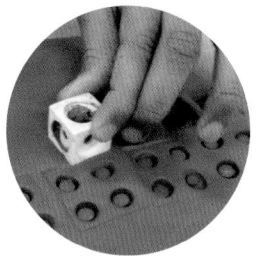

Newham, London. **Painting**: Wallands Community Primary School, Lewes, East Sussex. **Printing**: Peterborough High School, Junior Dept., Cambs.; Alix Critchley. P.37, bottom right, taken from *Handmade Prints* © Anne Desmet and Jim Anderson. **Collage & Textiles**: St Aloysius' Catholic Primary School, Oxford; The Oratory Prep School, Reading, Berks.; Dr South's C of E Primary School, Islip, Oxon; Broadwater Manor School, Worthing, West Sussex, and artist Patricia Greaves. Heart Educational Supplies for Indian wood blocks. **Sculpture**: Sir Francis Drake Primary School & Deptford Park Primary School, both Lewisham, London. **Digital media**: Wilbury Primary School, Enfield, London; Parklee Community School & Sacred Heart RC Primary School, both Atherton, London.

The rights of the authors of this work have been asserted by them in accordance with the Copyright, Designs and Patents Act 1988.

Due to the nature of the web, the publisher cannot guarantee the content of links of any of the websites referred to in this book. It is the responsibility of the reader to assess the suitability of websites. Ensure you read and abide by the terms and conditions of websites when you use material from websites or links.

A CIP catalogue record for this book is available from the British Library.

Art Express was developed at a time of change. It builds upon the first national curriculum which established the underlying principles, content and practice of art education. However, it allows schools to take ownership of their own curriculum content and to tailor it for their specific needs. *Art Express* illustrates how high-quality subject teaching can still be used to underwrite the development and evolution of new curriculum practice and supports teachers' professional development. Core to this approach are the role of new media, the significance of cross-curricular areas of learning and the importance of drawing as a key element of learning. The series covers the primary concepts and key processes of art education via six content areas –

- ■ **Drawing**
- ■ **Painting**
- ■ **Printing**
- ■ **Collage & Textiles**
- ■ **Sculpture**
- ■ **Digital Media**

Philosophy

Art Express is underwritten by clear principles about the nature and role of art in education. Central to this lies the understanding of art education as a process of generating ideas, realising them in material form, and being able to talk about what was done and why. This is best expressed as a set of three principles underlying each unit and session. They are seen clearly in the consistent pattern of learning objectives and assessment outcomes. Such principles are not unique to art education, and teachers will recognise the broader areas of learning and the duties on school to prepare pupils for the experiences of later life.

The three principles are related to:

- ■ The development of ideas and creativity
- ■ The development of skills and mastery of processes
- ■ The development of knowledge encompassing art and cultures.

Art and Education

Art Express takes a broad view of education and the role that art can play. Its principles echo across the curriculum. They indicate how art can contribute to essential aspects of children's personal development such as creativity, independence, judgement and self-reflection.

Art Express includes regular opportunities to learn about and explore other cultures: celebrating different cultural traditions while avoiding outdated stereotypes that should no longer have a place in children's understanding of our multicultural world.

Other areas of learning

Other areas of learning

Other areas of learning

Design

Skills and processes

Ideas and creativity

Communication (Art education)

Knowledge evaluation and review

Arts

Culture

Other areas of learning

Other areas of learning

Other areas of learning

IN THE CLASSROOM

Teaching

The units in *Art Express* exemplify good practice in teaching. They are written to model progression from first-hand experimentation and the acquisition of skills and technical knowledge, towards applying what has been learned with new independence and purpose, enabling pupils to become self-aware and confident learners.

Planning

The *Art Express* units have sequential logic and may be used as a scheme of work. The units build upon prior learning – progression and continuity are built into the scheme. The programme for each year ensures that the breadth and balance of experience, skills and curriculum content is appropriate for the age range.

However, from the outset, the editorial board of *Art Express* has been anxious to create a model of practice that is open to change and modification by creative teachers. Teachers will find it easy to adapt units to fit in with local circumstances and curriculum. For instance, all units may be adapted for different age ranges, purposes and contexts.

Within *Art Express*, the units illustrate how planned learning is sequential and cumulative. They model the process of enquiry and experimentation that generates ideas and develops familiarity with materials. This in turn promotes purposeful ideas and plans, following these through, mastering skills and regular reviewing of progress.

Each unit contains a sequence of sessions. These are not necessarily lessons of a fixed length but separate learning segments. For instance, some of the sessions in the digital media units are a series of short episodes, each of which must be completed before moving on. Teachers can manage these in different ways – for example, by using small groups or by adapting material from one session to cover several weeks. Alternatively, an arts week could compress sessions within a short time-frame, possibly held across the school, with activities for each year group structured from their appropriate book.

Assessment

Art Express provides a good model for assessment of learning. It offers examples of what teachers should observe children do to confirm that they have made anticipated gains in learning. Units often plan explicitly for children to discuss their findings, especially via the plenary. This offers the opportunity to assess children's comprehension and to review the next steps. It also reinforces the expectation for children to become partners in the assessment of their own progress, and thus to become more independent learners.

Art Express supports the increasing emphasis upon personalised learning by giving practical suggestions for managing issues such as differentiation in addition to reflection opportunities and self-assessment rubrics.

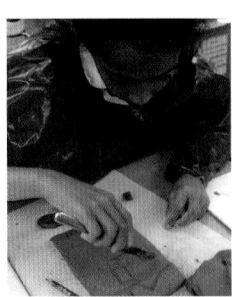
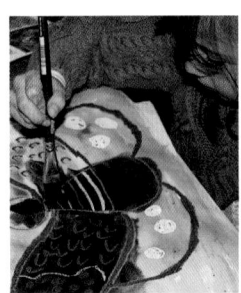

WHAT'S IN THE BOOKS

Each unit has an introduction page with key issues and aims for the topic. Double-page spreads contain full instructions for carrying out each session, including learning objectives and assessment for learning. Other areas of learning (left) offers ideas for extending the topic across the curriculum. Images on session pages (below) show examples of work from children who have trialled each project.

UNITS

The units in *Art Express* illustrate teaching and learning within six areas of experience – Painting, Printing, Sculpture, Collage & Textiles, Drawing and Digital Media. The first four units support learning through the progressive development of experience, skills and knowledge.

Drawing is seen as a key skill that underwrites all activity in art, and most units include it as ideas and plans are developed and revised. The drawing units themselves provide a complementary approach and can often be used in conjunction with other units. As stand-alone units, they focus on drawing as a means of perception, invention and communication and involve drawing from observation, memory and imagination.

Similarly, the digital media units have a dual role, in that the techniques and processes can be adapted and incorporated directly into the other units as part of exploring and developing ideas. Most of the digital media units seek to engage children directly with some first-hand experience of materials, and outcomes are often a combination of digital plus practical skills and techniques and demonstrate how digital media may be used creatively to support learning through art.

The units of work have been developed to support good practice in planning and assessment and in challenging children to reach high standards and to use their creativity and imagination. They also provide clear and practical advice and guidance on teaching the skills and techniques that children will need to master in order to achieve success.

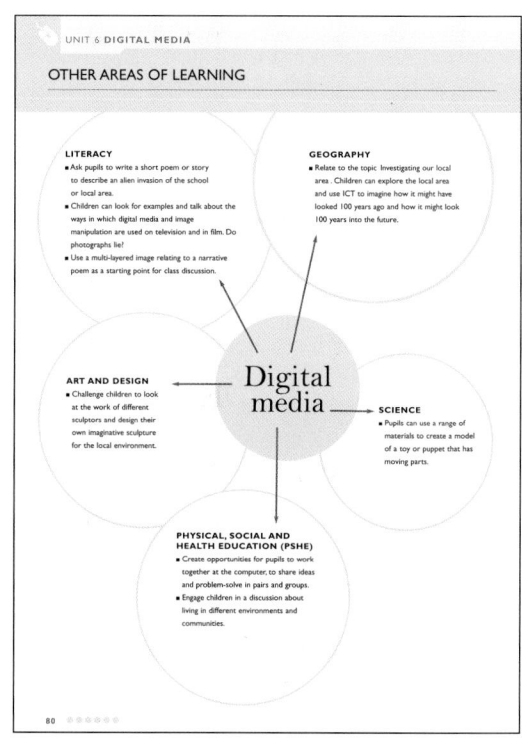

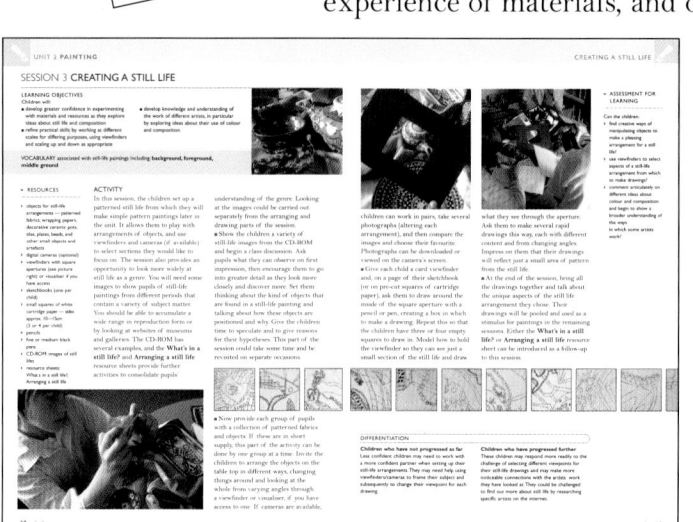

WHAT'S ON THE CD-ROM

The following supporting materials are available on the CD-ROM:

- Resource sheets – photocopiable and whiteboard resources for pupils and teachers
- Teacher assessment sheet per unit
- Pupil self-evaluation sheet per unit
- *PowerPoint* presentations
- Image library of Artists' works
- Library of reference images
- Image library of Children's work from trial schools
- Virtual gallery with specially commissioned software to allow uploading of pupils' work
- Teachers reference including 'Skills and Processes' chart, list of suppliers and session-by-session unit vocabulary.

RESOURCES

Art Express provides a range of additional resources for teachers and children on the complementary CD-ROM. Teachers will find these resources inspire and illuminate learning by presenting exciting visual examples and references. These resources are starting points, examples and signposts – teachers will find many more resources locally and will adapt these to expand the collection.

Viewing art on screen from disks or the internet brings opportunities to

see many large, bright images of art, craft and design. Wherever possible, teachers should also lead their pupils to first-hand or hands-on experience of real arts, bringing artefacts into the classroom and organising outings to local art galleries and museums.

Finally, the CD-ROM contains an interactive **Virtual Gallery** – specially created software that will enable children to build their own art galleries to support reflection and discussion, and to celebrate the individual work of the school.

Above and left
Image library, including images of children's work.

Left
PowerPoint presentations include information and demonstrations for teachers and pupils.

Far left and centre
Photocopiable and whiteboard resources for pupils and teachers.

Left
Pupil self-evaluation and teacher assessment sheets support each unit.

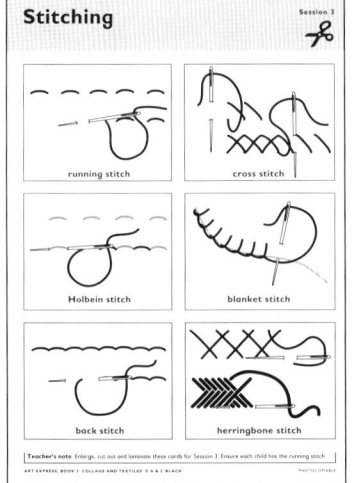

7

HOW TO USE THE CD-ROM

GETTING STARTED
- **PC**: the *Art Express* programme should auto-run when you insert the CD-ROM. If not, use My Computer to browse the contents of the CD-ROM and click on the File setup.
- **Mac**: insert the CD-ROM and double-click the *Art Express* icon. Open the folder and double-click the *Art Express* icon inside.

NETWORKING
Schools that have purchased a site licence are permitted to install and save the CD-ROM on a server and allow access on workstations within the school. Out-of-school access is not permitted, and image download permissions remain as above.

Use the MSI installer to deploy *Art Express* if you have a suitable network, or install *Art Express* to a server using the method described in Getting Started. Then, at each workstation, browse to the Installation folder on the server and run the File setup. Follow the instructions to create a shortcut to *Art Express* on the workstation.

TECHNICAL SUPPORT
Email A&C Black Customer Services on educationalsales@acblack.com.

MINIMUM SPECIFICATION
- PC with CD-ROM drive:
  Windows 98, 2000, XP or Vista
- Processor: Pentium 2 (or equivalent),
  1GHz
- Ram: 256 MB
- Graphics: 800 x 600, 16-bit display,
  3D accelerator (recommended)
- Mac with CD-ROM drive:
  OS X 10.1.5 and above
- Processor: G4 1GHz
- Ram: 256 MB
- Graphics: 800 x 600, 16-bit display,
- 3D accelerator (recommended)

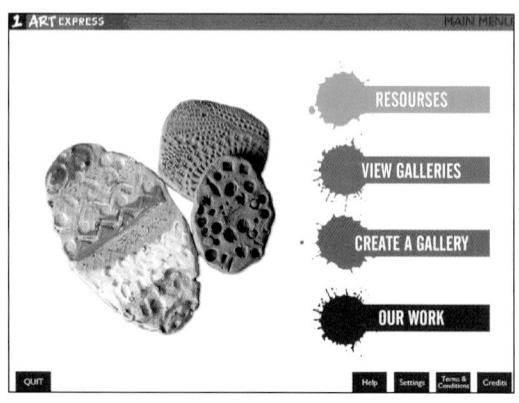

CD-ROM NAVIGATION
Main menu
From the main menu, teachers can access each of the following areas of the CD:

1. Teacher Resources
Access the bank of artist's and children's work, photos and videos, plus PDF and PowerPoint resources. Also view the artwork that you import from other sources.

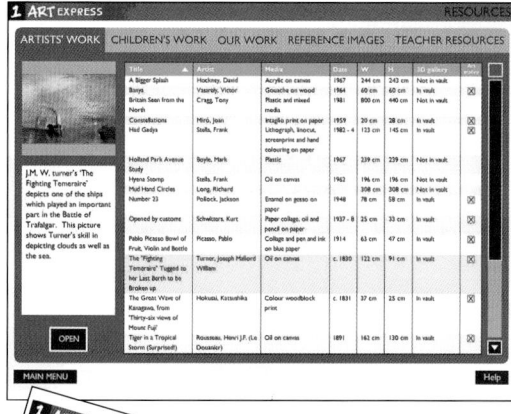

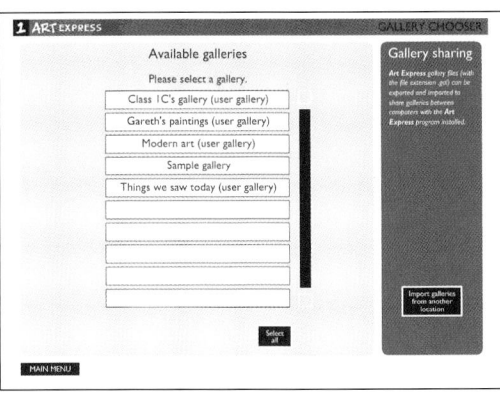

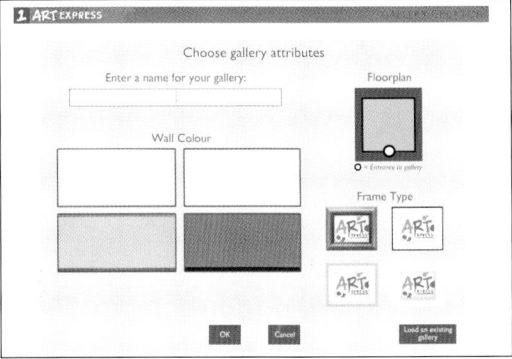

2. View Galleries

View the default virtual 3D galleries, together with the ones that you create. In this book there is only one pre-set gallery.

3. Create a Gallery

Use this to create your own virtual 3D gallery. Choose your floorplan, wall colour and framing theme, then get artist's work from the vault – or your own imported artwork – and position the pieces on the walls.

4. Our work

Use this to import image files into the programme to use in a virtual gallery or transfer them to another computer with *Art Express* installed.

1. Teacher Resources Menu

Once in the Teacher Resources menu, the following resources are accessed:

a) Images

There are three types of images available on the CD-ROM:

- **Image library of Artists' work**
  These are specific images referred to in the sessions; some may be imported into the **Virtual Gallery**, but not all.
  Note: None of these images can be printed due to copyright provisions.

- **Library of reference images**
  These are additional images which may be referred to during sessions, or be used for reference or stimulus.

- **Image library of Children's work**
  These are images of work created by children during the trialling of the units in schools.

b) Resource sheets

Photocopiable and whiteboard resources for pupils and teachers.

c) Assessment sheets

Pupil self-evaluation and teacher assessment sheets support each unit.

d) Presentations

PowerPoint presentations for teachers and pupils, and masterclasses for teachers, which can be shared with pupils. (To alter or adapt the *PowerPoint* files, use these files stored in the folder on the CD-ROM.)

e) Teachers' planning

Includes a 'Skills and Processes' chart for longterm planning, a list of suppliers and session-by-session vocabulary for each unit.

DRAWING IS DIFFERENT

Art Express supports contemporary curriculum modelling and planning as well as providing detailed guidance and support for teaching. The units of work have been developed to support good practice in planning, assessment and challenging pupils to reach high standards and to use their creativity and imagination. They also provide clear and practical guidance on teaching the skills and techniques that children will need to master in order to achieve success.

Foundation skill

In *Art Express*, drawing is seen as a core skill that underpins all activity in art. Indeed, as ideas and plans are developed and revised, most units will indicate the significant role of drawing via perception, invention and communication.

The drawing units themselves bear witness to the philosophy that sees the production of drawing as an internal dialogue for making choices, judgements and decisions – via observation, memory and imagination. The development of this internal communication strategy runs through every activity and each unit.

Technique and development

In learning to draw, children will gain experience of a wide range of tools and materials. They will develop a range of strategies and learn how drawing can be used for different purposes. However, teachers are invited to see drawing not purely as a set of techniques, but as a process that has much to do with attitude, habit, the ability to make connections and, above all, to be creative.

Expert author

The drawing units have been written by Eileen Adams who initiated the Campaign for Drawing programme, which resulted in the Big Draw, and numerous publications that explore the role of drawing as an essential and intrinsic part of learning and as a strategy for thinking.

Cross-curricular application

The drawing units are presented in a similar way to the other units, but teachers should use the activities and techniques as means of enriching and extending thinking and learning – across the curriculum wherever children are invited to think, look, speculate, imagine and come up with fresh ideas.

These activities are presented for use with particular age ranges and can be followed sequentially to provide a rich and intensive experience of drawing. Creative teachers, however, will also see opportunities to use these ideas for lessons in other sequences, with other age ranges and in a variety of curriculum situations.

For more information about the campaign for drawing and the work of Eileen Adams, go to: www.campaignfordrawing.org/education/index.aspx

Drawing has been used throughout history to represent the world and make sense of it – it is an important means of thinking. It is not only making marks on paper to represent things; it is also understanding experience and ideas, and sharing that knowledge. Children draw to explore their world, to understand it and to communicate their ideas to others. Drawing creates a strong sense of engagement, together with a personal and emotional response.

Prior to Year 3, pupils will have had experience using varied tools and materials to make drawings for different purposes, and should be able to name them. They should find pleasure in trying new things and experimenting. Children should be accustomed to using drawing to explore, develop, refine and communicate ideas. Pupils in Year 3 should be able to draw from memory, observation and imagination. They should be inspired to explore and develop control over a variety of tools and media, investigate a range of marks, and choose particular tools and materials to make large and small drawings. They should be encouraged to look at drawings – their own and those of other people – and learn that different kinds of drawing have different purposes. They should be stimulated to talk about drawing and recognise how it can be used as a starting point for thinking about lots of different things.

The drawing units in *Art Express* focus on learning through drawing using five themes: place, nature, buildings, people and things in the children's immediate surroundings. In this unit, the focus is on what children do in school. They daydream, they play, they learn, they sit and chat to friends, they have lunch. It includes a range of drawing techniques that are used for different purposes: cartoon strip, diagram, annotated sketch, designs and graph.

AIMS
This unit offers children the opportunity to:
- use drawing to observe, analyse, investigate, invent and communicate ideas and information
- experiment and investigate different tools and surfaces in order to make appropriate choices
- develop skills using a wide range of marks with varied angle, speed, pressure and sharpness to show line, tone, shape, pattern and texture
- use drawings to review, adapt and refine their ideas and those of others and recognise that artists and designers often use drawing as a starting point.
- look at, recognise and talk about drawings from different contexts and cultures and consider their purposes.

ASSESSMENT FOR LEARNING
Assessment should focus not only on how well the child can draw, but also on what the child learns through drawing – the knowledge, skills and attitudes that are developed through drawing. How well children can draw will be indicated by the confidence with which they engage in drawing activities, their skill in the use of tools and materials and discrimination in using appropriate drawing strategies. Cues for how well drawing is aiding the learning process will be in how the act of drawing prompts the child to reflect on experience, to question, to wonder and to generate ideas.

▶ CD-ROM RESOURCES
- Presentation: Drawing outside
- Artworks and images
- Resource sheets:
  - Ideas to go drawing… in school
  - Ideas to go drawing… at the beach
- Teacher assessment
- Pupil self-evaluation

11

SESSION | PEOPLE: PUT YOURSELF IN THE PICTURE

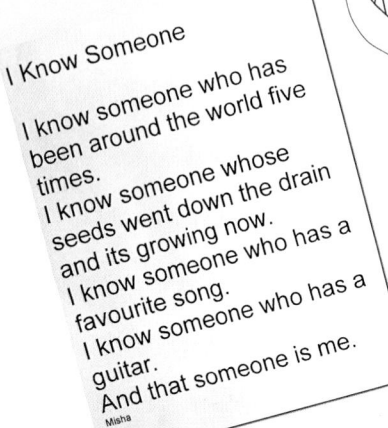

LEARNING OBJECTIVES

Children will:

- learn to observe, investigate, invent and communicate ideas and information by using drawing to present ideas
- develop imagination by recognising that drawing can be used to visualise and to develop initial ideas

- learn to experiment by making choices about, and using, different tools and surfaces
- develop further knowledge and understanding about different cultures by looking at and talking about drawings from different contexts and cultures.

VOCABULARY after, before, beginning, middle, end, next, story, happens, frame, cartoon, cartoon strip

▼ RESOURCES

- ▶ cartoon strips (some examples on the CD-Rom)
- ▶ A3 white paper
- ▶ pens and brushes
- ▶ coloured ink
- ▶ water
- ▶ resource sheets: Ideas to go drawing…

▼ ASSESSMENT FOR LEARNING

Can the children:

- ▶ use their drawings of people and situations to inform cartoon ideas?
- ▶ use a variety of tools and/ or surfaces in their work?
- ▶ talk about and comment on the cultural dimension of the work they are discussing as well as the visual appearance?

ACTIVITY

Show the children examples of cartoon strips. These can be found in comics, storybooks, newspapers and some school textbooks, or you could ask the children to bring in their own examples. Try to include cartoons from different contexts and cultures, some of which may be available on the internet. Discuss the content of the examples with the children and then move on to a discussion of the style of presentation. Lead the discussion towards an identification of key features and an understanding of the different contexts and cultures, if appropriate.

■ Discuss with the class the structure for the content of the story (what the story is about). For example, *The pictures tell a story. The story is divided into parts. It has a beginning, a middle*

I Know Someone

I know someone who has been around the world five times.
I know someone whose seeds went down the drain and its growing now.
I know someone who has a favourite song.
I know someone who has a guitar.
And that someone is me.

Misha

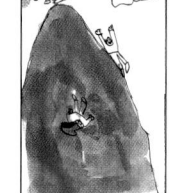

and an end. The story is funny. Then discuss the style of the story (how the story is presented). For example, *The parts of the story are presented in a series of frames. Drawings make use of simple lines and shapes. Each cartoon strip uses a particular set of colours – or only black and white.*

■ Tell the class about a funny thing that happened to you (real or imaginary), recounting the story in three parts. For example, *I was at the beach, sunbathing. My deckchair suddenly collapsed. The ice cream I was eating fell down the front of my bathing costume.*

■ Ask the children what funny things have happened to them and encourage them to explain the setting, the experience or action, and what happened as a result. Encourage all the children to participate, perhaps relating their incidents to a partner, rather than a group or the whole class.

■ Ask the children to decide on one

I Know Someone

I know someone who can bounce really high on the trampoline.
I know someone who likes to go on the tube.
I know someone who can ride a horse by trotting.
I know someone who can ride a two wheeled bike.
And that someone is me.

Lola

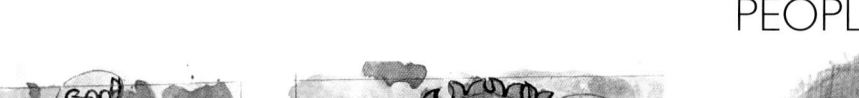

funny incident that happened to them that could be turned into a funny story – or they can make up a story and put themselves in the picture! They could choose to be, for example, a famous footballer, an Olympic cyclist or a ballroom dancer and imagine something funny happening to them. How can they show this in three picture frames? Ask the class to discuss possible scenarios and invite individual children to draw characters on the whiteboard, to stimulate thinking about the range of possibilities. Encourage the children to make some preliminary sketches to help refine their thinking for the three frames.

■ Give the children a grid of three frames to work on – each frame should have sides of at least 15cm. The grids could comprise three squares, two squares and a rectangle or three rectangles. To avoid the usual approach of drawing an outline and colouring it in, encourage the children to work with brushes and washes first, to establish basic shapes for people, places and things. When these are dry, lines can be added to define more clearly what the shapes represent.

■ In a plenary session, ask the children to show their strips to the class and to explain what they found difficult, or easy, in the process of creating their own cartoon strip. Ask, *Did you find it easy to choose an incident for the cartoon? How did you create only three frames from your incident? Compare your three frames with a partner. Would you change anything in your cartoon after looking at others? What would you change, and why?*

DIFFERENTIATION

Children who have not progressed as far...
Those who are less confident can experiment with making shapes, then changing them into something with the addition of a few lines.

Children who have progressed further...
Pupils who have tackled one cartoon strip confidently can create a sequel to show what happened next.

SESSION 2 **PLACE: GAME FOR A LAUGH**

LEARNING OBJECTIVES

Children will:

- learn to collect and select visual information and make drawings for different purposes
- develop imagination and creativity by using drawing to capture their ideas
- develop practical skills and confidence by experimenting with and using a variety of drawing tools and media.

VOCABULARY map, position, boundary, area, divide, mark, label, line, symbol

▼ RESOURCES

▸ A3 white paper
▸ marker pens
▸ felt-tip pens
▸ coloured chalks
▸ digital camera (optional)
▸ resource sheets: Ideas to go drawing…

▼ ASSESSMENT FOR LEARNING

Can the children:
▸ represent places accurately in a drawn map?
▸ draw a game, using their imagination?
▸ demonstrate increasing control over the drawing tools used?

ACTIVITY

In this session, pupils will choose a location in the school grounds and make up a game to play there. The session will easily break into two or more lessons, depending on the amount of time the children use to discuss and draft their new game. The exploration of the new game and the new environment can become the focus of the second lesson.

■ Take a walk around the school and ask the children to identify the different spaces and structures. Do the spaces have names – the playground, the quiet area, the garden? Can the children differentiate between the different buildings and classrooms? What are the boundaries – walls, fences, railings, hedges? What are the surfaces of the ground on which they are walking – tarmac, concrete, grass? They can make sketches in their sketchbooks.

■ Back in the classroom, ask the children to recall their walk and help you construct a sketch plan of the school site, checking with the sketches they made. Ask, *Where did we stop? What could we see from there? Where can we shelter if it rains? What is at the edge of the playground? Where is the main entrance to the school building? Where are the places in the playground that you prefer to go at break and lunchtime?*

■ Invite the children to identify the places they like and do not like, and discuss reasons. Ask them to say what games they play and identify where they play them. Encourage them to sketch pictures of children playing a variety of games. These can later be placed on a playground map.

■ Ask the children to refer to their sketchbooks and make drawings of their games. If these drawings are done with black pen on acetate or on an interactive whiteboard, you can use them in a class discussion to encourage pupils to reflect on their experience. The drawings can then be overlapped on a display board to create groups of figures playing.

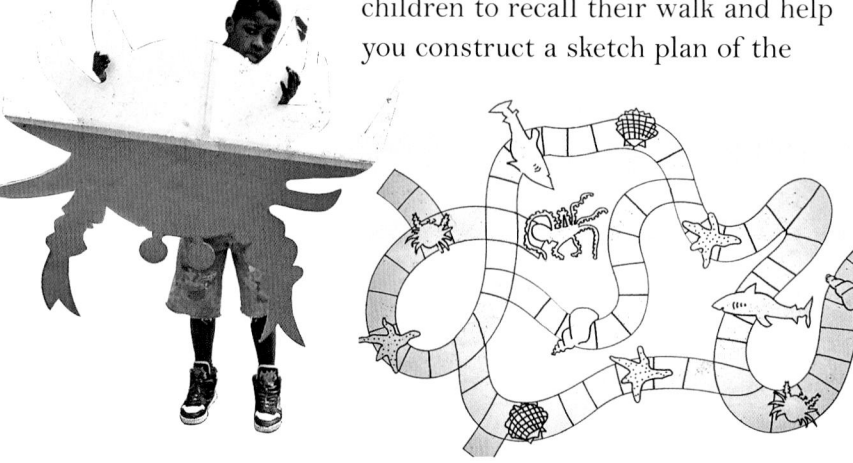

■ Ask the children to think of and discuss other kinds of games – prompt them to think about 'let's pretend' games that involve imagination and role-play. Ask them to think of a pretend game and a character they would like to be in the game – for example, an invisible person, a diver, a pirate or a dancer.

■ Take the class back to the playground to identify places that could be used for this kind of play. Ask each child to choose a place and make up a game to play there, creating an imaginary environment as a setting (such as a treasure island, a magic forest, under the sea, at the beach, a flower garden, a wildlife park). Using coloured chalks, challenge the children to draw on the playground a representation of what this place would be like. They should be encouraged to draw freely and quickly. Any lines or marks that are in the wrong place can be drawn over. The chalk drawings can be photographed for inclusion in their sketchbooks.

■ If time permits, or in a break time, encourage the children to play some of the games created by their classmates. Back in the classroom, ask them to relate how the games were played, and possibly suggest changes or improvements.

DIFFERENTIATION

Children who have not progressed as far…
Pupils who are not able to visualise an imaginary place should be given some questions and cues to start them off. What would they see in a magic forest? What would the trees look like? What animals would they find in the trees? What colours would the flowers be? What would they find if they went deep into the forest? They should be encouraged to draw what they see in their mind's eye.

Children who have progressed further…
Children who are able to imagine a place and represent it should be encouraged to describe what might happen there and to draw some actions and scenes from the place.

SESSION 3 **BUILDINGS: THE GOOD, THE BAD AND THE UGLY**

LEARNING OBJECTIVES

Children will:

- learn to explore and develop ideas for work by using drawing to communicate and share ideas in other media
- develop confidence in their ability to draw things they see, know and remember, and appreciate similarities and differences
- begin to develop and use drawing systems that enable depth to be shown.

VOCABULARY good, useful, beautiful, practical, bad, ugly, impractical, extend, change, improve

▼ RESOURCES

- ▶ digital cameras
- ▶ A3 paper
- ▶ glue
- ▶ felt-tip pens
- ▶ resource sheets: Ideas to go drawing…

▼ ASSESSMENT FOR LEARNING

Can the children:

- ▶ use a range of media when working on their drawing?
- ▶ add detail that demonstrates their memory of the building?
- ▶ make drawings and pictures that use simple techniques to show depth?

ACTIVITY

In this session, the children will photograph different views of the school and use parts of the images to create extended drawings.

■ Take the class for a walk around the school building. Invite the children to comment on all the things they notice about the building – the materials, its structure and decoration, how many windows there are and their shapes, where the doorways are and any interesting details. Some examples of school buildings are on the CD-ROM, if it is difficult to take children out.

■ Divide the class into groups and ask each group to choose a view of the building. One member of the group should take a photograph of the scene, for later reference. Challenge each group to say six things

about their chosen view, mentioning perhaps the materials, its size, colour, decorative details and what it reminds them of. Each child can then photograph an interesting part of the building and think about why they have chosen that particular detail or item.

■ Print out all the photographs and stick the children's own photos, showing specific details, onto A3 sheets. The children can then identify their own photograph and take that sheet to work on. Ask them to create a drawing of the scene, working from memory and using the photograph as a starting point. Show them how to extend the lines in their photograph onto the paper using felt-tip pens. These lines will begin to recreate the scene surrounding the detail they have photographed. Some children call this technique 'extender drawings'. If you stick the photograph onto the middle of the page, there will be room for the children to extend their drawing at the top, bottom and sides of the

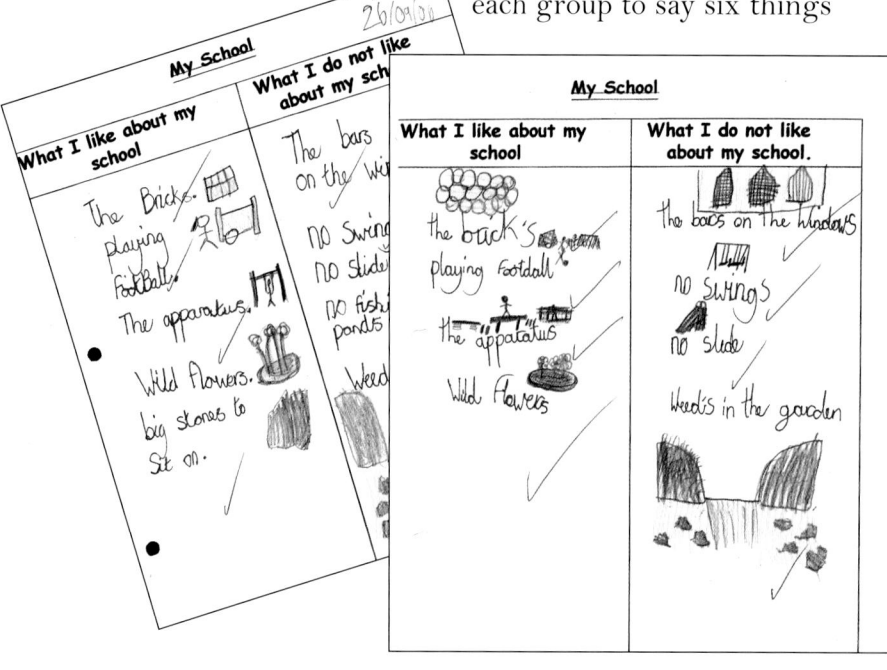

photograph. The drawing will reveal what children have noticed and remembered.

■ Invite the children to look again at the first photograph taken by their group of the whole scene and to compare it to their drawing. How many of the features visible in the photograph did they notice and include in their drawing? Ask them to look at each other's work and compare the different ways everyone has been able to recall information. Just as with writing and reading words, children get used to drawing and interpreting visual symbols.

■ Discuss with the children 'the good, the bad and the ugly' – things they think look good or work well (good); things they do not think are so good (bad); and things that could be easily improved (ugly). It is usually easy for children to say what they love or hate. However, it is important here for the

children to give reasons for their choices. For example: *This window is good because it opens to let air into the classroom. This fencing is bad because it makes the school look like a prison. These paving stones are ugly because they are cracked. They should be mended in case someone trips and falls.*

■ Their comments can be used as captions for the drawings. When displaying the drawings, you may wish to annotate them with questions to encourage other children to observe their surroundings more closely. Encourage the children to undertake further drawing tasks, such as those suggested in the **Ideas to go drawing…** resource sheets.

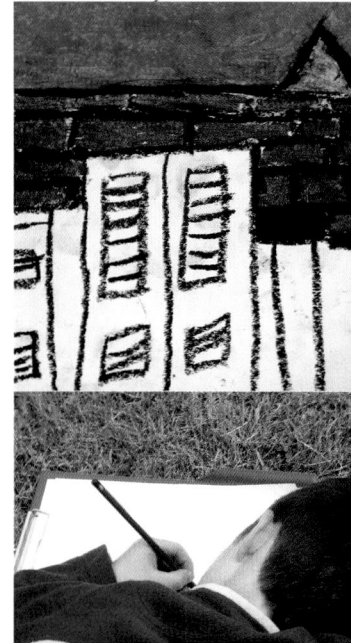

DIFFERENTIATION

Children who have not progressed as far…
Those children who have found the activities of recall and representation difficult should go with an adult to view the school building again and draw it from observation. Afterwards, they should be encouraged to describe what they saw.

Children who have progressed further…
Pupils who have tackled this drawing activity confidently can cover their extender drawings with acetate. This is fixed at one side with masking tape. Using felt-tip pens, they can draw onto the acetate anything they would change to improve the appearance of the school. They can lift the acetate up and down to show 'before' and 'after'.

SESSION 4 THINGS: SITTING AROUND

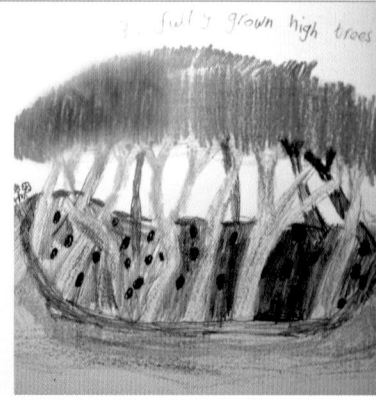

full grown high trees

LEARNING OBJECTIVES

Children will:

- learn to collect and experiment with ideas purposefully by using a sketchbook
- learn to experiment and investigate by trying different tools and surfaces in order to make appropriate choices

- learn to review, adapt and refine their ideas and those of others by using drawing to capture and represent thinking.

VOCABULARY seat, seating, bench, log, material, location, safety

▼ RESOURCES

- ▶ images of outdoor seating (some examples on the CD-Rom)
- ▶ paper in a variety of types and colours
- ▶ soft pencils
- ▶ crayons
- ▶ charcoal
- ▶ resource sheets: Ideas to go drawing…

▼ ASSESSMENT FOR LEARNING

Can the children:
- ▶ sketch variations on ideas and refer to sketches during their work?
- ▶ select and use a range of tools and materials that are appropriate for the drawing in hand?
- ▶ talk about their drawings, explain how they developed their seats and discuss with peers how they could be changed or improved?

ACTIVITY

In this session, pupils will consider seating in the school grounds and design a seat that can also be used for another purpose, such as climbing, sleeping or playing.

■ Following their exploration of the school grounds in Session 3, ask the children to discuss any outdoor seating. They might consider: *Where can pupils sit and rest? Where are other places that seating could be placed? Is there any shelter from rain and sun? Is it a safe place where people will not be hit by balls? Are there quiet places where they can read or talk?* Encourage them to discuss the pros and cons of seating and to use their own experiences of break time and how the school grounds are used, to think about what need there is for outdoor seating.

■ Show the children some examples from magazines, catalogues and the internet of ready-made seating, such as park benches, garden furniture and pub tables.

■ Move the discussion on to what is involved in designing seating – for example, location, shelter or safety. Mention that as well as having a seat for sitting on, children may climb, lie, crawl or stand on the seat and it needs to be strong to cope with this.

■ Invite the children to choose an object, such as a box, tube, crate or toy animal, and use it as a basis for a design for a seat in the school grounds. Ask them to draw the object, then make changes to it, to make it suitable for outdoor seating. The first drawing could be in one colour and the changes made to it in another colour. The drawing may have the feel of a

diagram. You can help the children annotate their drawings to draw attention to any special features.

■ Then ask the children to make a second drawing, an illustration, to show where their seat will be placed and how it will be used. The addition of figures to the drawing will give an idea of scale – how big the seat will be and how many pupils can use it. What will the seat be used for: climbing on, as a lookout; for lying on, to have a rest; or for sitting on to eat and talk to friends?

■ Display and discuss the drawings. Invite the children to explain their ideas and ask the rest of the class to comment on how well their ideas work. Revisit ideas about location, shelter and safety. Ask the children to reflect on the process they used in the

session: *What did you think about when you began the session? What questions did you have? How did you get the information you needed? Did you change your plan? What influenced your change of plan? How does your finished drawing compare to your original idea? What would you change now?*

■ The drawing activity can be a starting point for the children to make models of their seats using found or waste materials. Drawing creates time for thinking about the possibilities, exploring ideas and planning. Building the model develops an understanding of how parts fit together, and testing out how the thing will work.

■ Encourage the children to undertake further drawing tasks, such as those in the **Ideas to go drawing**… resource sheets.

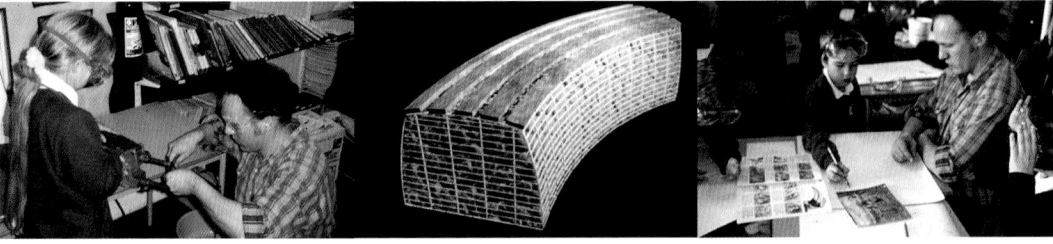

DIFFERENTIATION

Children who have not progressed as far…
Those children who are less confident can practise changing shapes, such as circles, ovals and rectangles, into something else.

Children who have progressed further…
Pupils who are confident in designing can be challenged to show what the seat looks like from the front, the side, the back and looking down on it. Some might be encouraged to develop a fixed number of further versions and variations on their idea.

SESSION 5 NATURE: WHAT'S FOR LUNCH?

LEARNING OBJECTIVES

Children will:

- gain confidence in the ability to explore and develop ideas for work in other media by using drawing to capture thoughts and ideas
- develop practical skills by using a wide range of marks with varied angle, speed, pressure and sharpness

- develop further understanding of the working process of artists by recognising that artists often use drawing as a starting point for work they might carry out in other media.

VOCABULARY fruit, vegetables, meat, fish, wheat, sugar, salt, water, lunchbox

▼ RESOURCES

- ▸ children's lunchboxes
- ▸ A3 white and coloured paper
- ▸ oil pastels
- ▸ A1 paper with grid drawn of different categories of food containing: meat, fish, fruit, vegetables, wheat, sugar and water (one per group)
- ▸ felt-tip pens
- ▸ citrus fruit and/or kiwi fruit
- ▸ books and magazines containing photographs of fruit
- ▸ pupil self-evaluation sheet

▼ ASSESSMENT FOR LEARNING

Can the children:

- ▸ show initial drawings used as inspiration for work in other media?
- ▸ show increasing sensitivity and control of marks used in their work?
- ▸ talk about the drawings of artists and comment on their use of drawings to show ideas and feelings?

ACTIVITY

In this session, pupils will study the food in their lunchboxes. If some children have packed lunch and others have school lunch, the children should work in pairs. If most have school lunch, they should invent a 'healthy lunchbox'.

■ Ask the children to discuss the different types of food in the lunchbox. Encourage them to also talk about their favourite foods and foods that are part of healthy eating: *I drink orange juice in the morning. I eat toast and honey. Sometimes I eat sweets and sometimes I eat raisins. I like banana sandwiches.*

■ Give each pair a piece of A3 paper and oil pastels and ask them to draw each item in the lunchbox (for example, a banana or tomato, crisps, sandwich). Encourage them to discuss the scale of each item and to reflect this in their drawings. As they are drawing their items, they should continue to discuss how they are

representing each item. Some children may be capable of adding three-dimensional effects to their drawings; others may not. When they have finished, ask them to cut out each item.

■ Place the children (or pairs) into groups of six or eight. Ask them to discuss (with an adult) each item: are they fruit or vegetable, meat or fish, do they contain wheat or sugar? Ask them to take their cut-out drawings and place them on the A1 grid according to type of food (see Resources). This activity involves skills of analysis and categorisation. Some food will fit into more than one category, such as ham sandwiches, and there may be other categories the group chooses to add, such as dairy products. When they have decided on what fits into which category, the drawings should be stuck down.

■ Display each group's chart and make comparisons: *this group likes fruit; that group eats a lot of cheese sandwiches; this other group is the only one that has included fish.* (A similar graph could be made for school lunch. A comparison could be made between the charts and graphs to inform discussions about healthy eating.)

■ Place the children in groups of up to six and give each group half a citrus fruit and/or a kiwi fruit. Ask them to observe the cut surface of the fruit and discuss the pattern and the texture they see. Then ask each child to draw the surface, showing as much detail as possible and use in a classroom display.

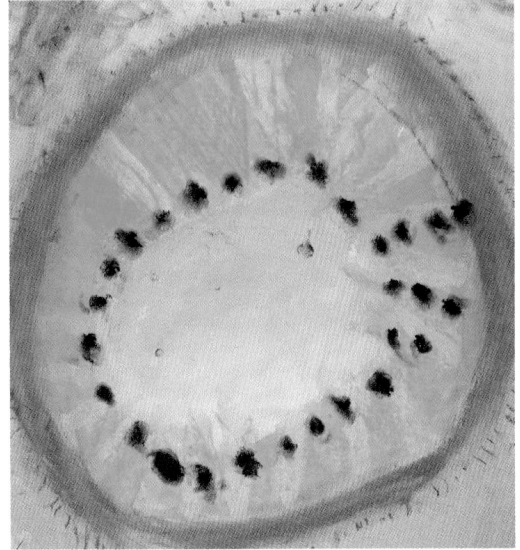

■ Provide the class with books and magazines containing photographs of fruit and vegetables, and ask the children to look in the class and school libraries for more examples. Compare drawings of fruit by artists, such as Cézanne's apples, with illustrations of fruit and vegetables in cookery books and advertisements that use stylised forms. Draw the children's attention to the distinctive shapes of fruit and vegetables, their colours and surface quality and the different ways artists and illustrators have represented them.

■ At the end of the session, provide each child with a **Pupil self-evaluation** sheet for feedback on the work undertaken in the unit.

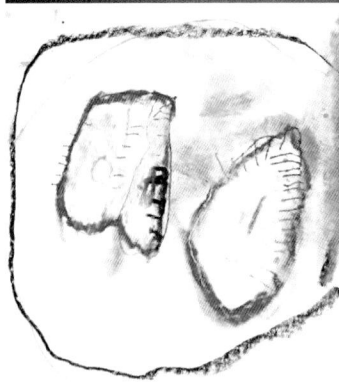

DIFFERENTIATION

Children who have not progressed as far...
Pupils who find it difficult to identify and categorise foods should be helped with their vocabulary.

Children who have progressed further...
Those children who have enjoyed this activity should be encouraged to create a menu for a healthy lunch. The menu should be a folded card with an illustration of food on the front and a written menu inside. Alternatively, they can be encouraged to cut up fruit and draw cross-sections from observation.

OTHER AREAS OF LEARNING

ART AND DESIGN

■ Ask the children to make a five-fruits 'healthy eating' badge. They can draw types of fruit on A3 coloured paper using black felt-tip pens, colour them in, then cut them out and stick them onto white paper to make a smiley face badge – oranges or apples for eyes, a pear for a nose, a banana for a mouth and grapes for hair!

■ Pupils could design invitations, stalls, tents and fancy-dress costumes for a summer fair to be held in the school grounds.

PHYSICAL, SOCIAL AND HEALTH EDUCATION (PSHE)

■ Encourage pupils to play cooperatively, learn to take turns, work together and help each other. Working in pairs in the playground, pupils can take turns to direct each other to create a chalk drawing. They can then work together to link their two drawings.

■ Ask pupils to work together to make a fresh fruit salad and serve it at lunch time.

MATHEMATICS

■ Pupils can make a survey of games played in the playground by boys and girls, and by different age groups, and use drawing to tabulate the results.

LITERACY

■ Pupils can experiment with materials to create different kinds and qualities of line, tone and texture. They can make connections between visual and verbal language, for example: line – short, long, straight, curved, wavy, dotted; tone – deep, strong, light, pale; texture – rough, smooth, bumpy, coarse.

■ Pupils can look at the illustrations in storybooks and information books about children from different countries. They can read stories to find out about their lives and use drawing to imagine the places and the people who live there.

Drawing

ICT

■ Pupils can scan in one of their line drawings. Using a simple drawing programme, they can add lines and experiment with different colours and effects to create a lively scene.

GEOGRAPHY

■ Challenge pupils to draw a large-scale map of the school grounds that shows how the grounds are used, and where different activities take place.

SCIENCE

■ Pupils can identify the materials that things are made of and use drawing to record them. For example, buttons may be made of plastic, wood or metal; cloth may be woven or printed.

■ Pupils could then choose appropriate drawing materials to explore different-shaped buttons and different kinds of textiles, such as woven and printed.

Painting is a key area of art and design practice and pupils should have frequent opportunities to engage with it. To paint with confidence, they need time to explore its liquid qualities, to experience different ways of applying it, to gain an appreciation of colour and to develop mastery of mixing the shades they need to realise their intentions.

Prior to Year 3, pupils should have experienced a broad range of painting activities, working with different paints and on various scales. During Years 1 and 2, they will have explored the tactile qualities of paint, moved from randomly mixing colour to discovering how particular shades are made and developed early skills with a range of painting implements. In the painting unit of *Art Express* Book 2, pupils learned to make secondary colours from a limited palette, to match specific shades and describe their differences and to consolidate their understanding of the consistency of paint. They painted imaginatively and from observation of natural pattern and applied their skills to a group painting.

This unit aims to provide further opportunities for the children to work in sketchbooks and on different scales, and to increase their skills in mixing and applying colour. Pattern provides the context for most of the unit, in which they mix secondary colours from a limited palette and use a range of paints and painting styles. They compare and contrast patterned works of art from different times and places. Small-scale watercolour work is contrasted with bold paintings, using poster paints, inks and marker pens on a large scale. The children make an arrangement of patterned objects and use viewfinders to select and isolate details for a still-life painting. The activities are presented as open-ended challenges so pupils can develop their own individual responses, and it is expected that the outcomes will all look different.

AIMS

This unit offers children the opportunity to:

- experiment with different approaches to using and applying paint
- freely explore ideas, working from first-hand experience, memory and imagination
- develop increased confidence in colour-mixing and mark-making, working with a wider range of paints and painting tools
- talk about colour and composition in their own and in artists' paintings, expressing opinions with appropriate vocabulary
- adapt and refine their own work, sharing ideas with others
- compare and contrast works of art from different times and places.

ASSESSMENT FOR LEARNING

This unit provides frequent opportunities to assess pupils' progress as they gain experience of painting in different ways. Teachers should note the ease with which they make informed choices of tools and media, mix the colours they need and decide on the composition of their painting. Teachers can look for specific evidence to show understanding of different materials and how they can be used, and pupils' capacity to critically view their own work using relevant vocabulary.

▶ CD-ROM RESOURCES

Artworks and images
Resource sheets:
    Making your mark
    What's in a still life?
    Arranging a still life
Teacher assessment
Pupil self-evaluation

SESSION 1 INVESTIGATING PATTERNS

LEARNING OBJECTIVES

Children will:

- develop practical skills by working from first-hand experience of textiles and images, exploring mark-making
- learn about patterns observed in a variety of stimulus material, using an appropriate vocabulary to describe them
- develop their capacity to reflect and improve by making refinements to their own work, having discussed and shared ideas with others.

VOCABULARY associated with describing pattern, such as **regular, irregular, geometric, abstract, natural, bold, delicate, detailed, embroidered, stitched, layered**

▼ RESOURCES

- ▶ an assortment of patterned fabrics, such as Indian embroidered, paisley, Art Nouveau, contemporary, geometric, floral (some examples on the CD-ROM)
- ▶ reproductions of fabrics or paintings including pattern, such as any Arts and Crafts (William Morris, Charles Voysey, Charles Rennie Mackintosh, MP Verneuil and so on), Klimt, Matisse, Hundertwasser. (Some examples on the CD-ROM)
- ▶ reference books about patterns and derivation, such as *1000 Patterns* by Drusilla Cole (A&C Black, available from libraries)
- ▶ a selection of black pens including fine, medium and broad-tipped
- ▶ sketchbooks (one per child)
- ▶ viewfinders – pieces of card with a small square or rectangle cut out for the children to look through
- ▶ tracing paper and glue sticks (optional)

ACTIVITY

In this first session, pupils are introduced to pattern through exposure to images and textiles. In advance of the session, collect examples of patterned fabrics (if possible, those mentioned in Resources), decorative objects, patterned paintings or prints. The focus of the session is on developing children's awareness of pattern and recording examples of it through a series of drawings in sketchbooks. Make a display of fabric swatches, postcards or downloaded images on each table or on the floor in the centre of the room for pupils to share.

■ Ask the children to look at the display, and give them some time to think and talk about what they can see. Through open-ended questioning, draw their attention to recurrent themes within the textiles or images you are showing them – the repeated appearance of animals, geometric shapes, plant forms; the regularity (or

irregularity) of the pattern; the bright or muted colours; the use of gold decoration and so on. Invite pupils to speculate about where the patterns come from and what might have inspired them, and ask them to describe shapes and motifs they see. Encourage the use of appropriate language to describe the different kinds of pattern and the colours they observe.

■ Distribute some black water-based pens in a range of sizes so that each table has a variety. Ask the children to choose a pen and a small area of pattern they can see, and then make a quick drawing of it in their sketchbook. Emphasise the idea of being selective and offer them viewfinders, modelling how to use them to isolate a small area at a time. Stress that the children are going to make a lot of drawings across their page, capturing different types of pattern, and that they should not get

bogged down with minute detail. After a short time (no more than two or three minutes), move the children on to a second drawing – a new pen and a different pattern – and then a third and so on. Talk to them about the sections they chose and their choice of pen with which to record it. Look for pupils' recognition that small, fiddly details are best drawn with fine-nibbed pens and bolder areas with thicker ones.

■ Stop the children when they have made four or five drawings. Ask them to swap books with someone else and have a mini-plenary discussion with the class. Invite them to identify a drawing that they especially like and to say why. Now ask them to copy that drawing in a space on their own page. Alternatively, you could photocopy the sketchbook pages and let them tear a section from someone else's page and stick it on their own (or trace a section if tracing paper is provided). This

conveys a positive message about everyone's achievements being valued and helps to build children's confidence.

■ Pupils should continue making rapid drawings until the double pages are full. Then ask them all to bring their open books together to talk about what they have recorded. Photocopy the children's pages as these will be used in the next session.

▼ ASSESSMENT FOR LEARNING

Can the children:
▶ make informed choices about which tools to use for particular purposes?
▶ contribute to a conversation about the qualities of different patterns and use appropriate words to describe them?
▶ adapt their own work in the light of sharing thoughts and ideas with other children?

DIFFERENTIATION

Children who have not progressed as far…
These pupils may benefit from advice about the different qualities of pattern to explore and how to change the focus of the drawing each time. They may also need help in using viewfinders and selecting appropriate pen sizes for recording particular kinds of pattern.

Children who have progressed further…
These children may respond more readily to the idea of making several different kinds of drawing and of using viewfinders to select detail. They may need additional time to make more complex arrangements of drawings and may use a more sophisticated vocabulary to describe patterns made and observed.

SESSION 2 COLOUR STUDIES

LEARNING OBJECTIVES

Children will:

- develop confidence and creativity by experimenting with approaches to applying paint in different ways, and increase their awareness of how it can be used

- consolidate and develop practical skills by exploring and developing increased competence in mark-making and colour-mixing with watercolour paints.

VOCABULARY shades of a colour: **pinkish-red, ruby red, raspberry, scarlet, orangey-red, lighter, darker, deeper**; describing the consistency, strength and application of watercolour paint: **watery, intense, transparent, strong, opaque, wash**

▼ RESOURCES

- ▶ sketchbooks (one per child)
- ▶ watercolour tins
- ▶ plastic or paper plates, ice-cream tub lids or other suitable large surfaces to mix paint
- ▶ brushes – good-quality fine nylon brushes
- ▶ water containers and sponges, rags or paper towels to dry brushes on
- ▶ photocopied sketchbook pages from Session 1
- ▶ resource sheet: Making your mark

ACTIVITY

In this session, pupils revisit some basic mark-making and colour-mixing tasks, using watercolour paints. The activity could be carried out in one sitting or, as it has two distinct parts, broken down into shorter sessions.

■ Demonstrate to the children how to make thin washes or more intense strengths of colour by either lightly brushing the surface of the colour tablet with a damp brush or running the brush back and forth over it for longer, until the paint takes on a creamy consistency. Pupils will need to practise this, especially if they have not used watercolours before. Ask them to choose a single strong colour (red, blue

or green work well) and challenge them to make a thin, watery wash followed by gradually stronger and more intense versions of that colour across a double page of their sketchbook.

■ Show them that they can hold their brush in different ways to make a range of marks. Model using the tip or the side of the brush or hold it at varying angles – each way will allow different kinds of marks to be made. Encourage them to try dragging their brush lightly, pressing more heavily, dabbing, sweeping and dotting colour onto the page. Regularly stop the class and draw their attention to marks that some children have made. The **Making your mark** resource sheet can be used as a prompt sheet (in paper form or projected onto an interactive

whiteboard), either as part of this activity or after the session as a follow-up.

■ Talk about shades of colour and remind pupils of the basic principles of colour-mixing. Show them that by adding tiny touches of other colours, they can greatly extend the range of shades available of their chosen colour. Describe the colours they could make, such as greeny-blue, sky blue, purplish-blue, turquoise or midnight blue by adding dabs of red or yellow to the two shades of blue tablets supplied in the watercolour tin. Challenge the children to fill the remaining spaces on their sketchbook page with as many new shades of their principal colour as possible.

■ Now give each child a photocopy of the double-page spread of drawings they made in Session 1. Ask them to mix lots of shades of their chosen colour and to use these to paint small sections of their drawings. (They will

need to work from photocopies to avoid the paint smudging their original drawings.) This is an opportunity to practise their brush skills, as well as to consolidate their experience of mixing a wide range of colours and applying paint in different consistencies. Encourage pupils to choose different-sized brushes as appropriate and to mix intense colour, thin washes and strengths in between. Use some of the words suggested in Vocabulary above to reinforce the skills they are developing. At the end of the session, make time for the children to talk together about their work and express views on how it could be improved.

▼ ASSESSMENT FOR LEARNING

▸ produce a wide range of experimental marks and patterns in their sketchbooks, using watercolour paints in different opacities?

▸ mix an extensive range of shades of the same colour, and match, describe and name them?

DIFFERENTIATION

Children who have not progressed as far…
These children may need help with modelling some of the marks and colours they can make, and may produce a less extensive range. Working in pairs would give them a partner with whom to share discoveries or the **Making your mark** resource sheet could be simplified for them.

Children who have progressed further…
These pupils may make an extensive range of marks and colours and assimilate more readily ideas observed in others' work. They may describe the choices they are making with a more developed vocabulary and could be provided with some specific questions to guide their discoveries.

SESSION 3 CREATING A STILL LIFE

LEARNING OBJECTIVES

Children will:

- develop greater confidence in experimenting with materials and resources as they explore ideas about still life and composition
- refine practical skills by working at different scales for differing purposes, using viewfinders and scaling up and down as appropriate
- develop knowledge and understanding of the work of different artists, in particular by exploring ideas about their use of colour and composition.

VOCABULARY associated with still-life paintings including: **background, foreground, middle ground**

▼ RESOURCES

- ▶ objects for still-life arrangements – patterned fabrics, wrapping papers, decorative ceramic pots, tiles, plates, beads, and other small objects
- ▶ digital cameras (optional)
- ▶ viewfinders with square apertures (see picture right) or visualiser if you have access
- ▶ sketchbooks (one per child)
- ▶ small squares of white cartridge paper – sides approx. 10–15cm (3 or 4 per child)
- ▶ pencils
- ▶ fine or medium black pens
- ▶ CD-ROM: images of still lifes
- ▶ resource sheets: What's in a still life?; Arranging a still life

ACTIVITY

In this session, the children set up a patterned still life from which they will make simple pattern paintings later in the unit. It allows them to play with arrangements of objects, and use viewfinders and cameras (if available) to select sections they would like to focus on. The session also provides an opportunity to look more widely at still life as a genre. You will need some images to show pupils of still-life paintings from different periods that contain a variety of subject matter. You should be able to accumulate a wide range in reproduction form or by looking at websites of museums and galleries. The CD-ROM has several examples, and the **What's in a still life?** and **Arranging a still life** resource sheets provide further activities to consolidate pupils'

understanding of the genre. Looking at the images could be carried out separately from the arranging and drawing parts of the session.

- Show the children a variety of still-life images from the CD-ROM and begin a class discussion. Ask pupils what they can observe on first impression, then encourage them to go into greater detail as they look more closely and discover more. Set them thinking about the kind of objects that are found in a still-life painting and talking about how these objects are positioned and why. Give the children time to speculate and to give reasons for their hypotheses. This part of the session could take some time and be revisited on separate occasions.

 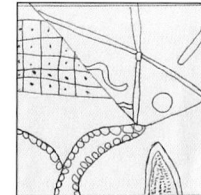 

- Now provide each group of pupils with a collection of patterned fabrics and objects. If these are in short supply, this part of the activity can be done by one group at a time. Invite the children to arrange the objects on the table top in different ways, changing things around and looking at the whole from varying angles through a viewfinder or visualiser, if you have access to one. If cameras are available,

Can the children:
▶ find creative ways
  of manipulating objects
  to make a pleasing
  arrangement for a
  still life?
▶ use viewfinders to select
  aspects of a still-life
  arrangement from which
  to make drawings?
▶ comment articulately
  on different ideas about
  colour and composition
  and begin to show a
  broader understanding
  of the ways in which
  some artists work?

children can work in pairs, take several photographs (altering each arrangement), and then compare the images and choose their favourite. Photographs can be downloaded or viewed on the camera's screen.

■ Give each child a card viewfinder and, on a page of their sketchbook (or on pre-cut squares of cartridge paper), ask them to draw around the inside of the square aperture with a pencil or pen, creating a box in which to make a drawing. Repeat this so that the children have three or four empty squares to draw in. Model how to hold the viewfinder so they can see just a small section of the still life and draw

what they see through the aperture. Ask them to make several rapid drawings this way, each with different content and from changing angles. Impress on them that their drawings will reflect just a small area of pattern from the still life.

■ At the end of the session, bring all the drawings together and talk about the unique aspects of the still life arrangement they chose. Their drawings will be pooled and used as a stimulus for paintings in the remaining sessions. Either the **What's in a still life?** or **Arranging a still life** resource sheet can be introduced as a follow-up to this session.

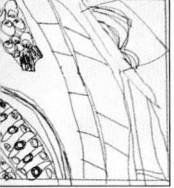 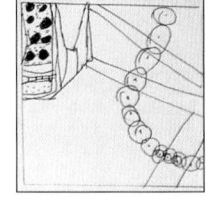 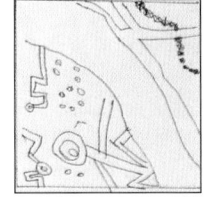 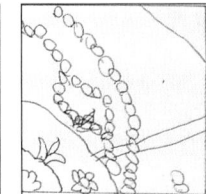 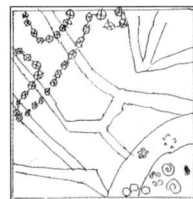 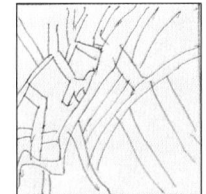 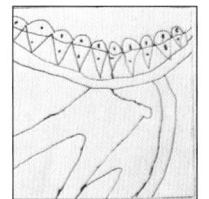

DIFFERENTIATION

Children who have not progressed as far...
Less confident children may need to work with a more confident partner when setting up their still-life arrangements. They may need help using viewfinders/cameras to frame their subject and subsequently to change their viewpoint for each drawing.

Children who have progressed further...
These children may respond more readily to the challenge of selecting different viewpoints for their still-life drawings and may make more noticeable connections with the artists' work they have looked at. They could be challenged to find out more about still life by researching specific artists on the internet.

SESSION 4 PAINTINGS LARGE AND SMALL 1

LEARNING OBJECTIVES

Children will:

- learn to experiment purposefully with ideas, and explore ways of selecting shapes and patterns to make compositions that suit their intentions
- develop further practical skills of mixing and applying colour
- learn to reflect on their own work and the work of other children, and consider how it might be adapted and refined.

VOCABULARY associated with the opacity of paint, ways of applying it and changing colours: **watery**, **translucent**, **matt**, **opaque**, **tone**, **tint**, **shade**

▼ RESOURCES

- ▸ viewfinder drawings from Session 3
- ▸ small squares of watercolour paper (or good-quality heavyweight cartridge paper) – with sides approximately 15–20cm
- ▸ sketchbooks (optional)
- ▸ soft pencils
- ▸ watercolour tins
- ▸ plastic or paper plates, ice-cream tub lids or other suitable large surfaces to mix paint
- ▸ fine nylon brushes (as before)
- ▸ water containers and sponges, rags or paper towels to dry brushes on

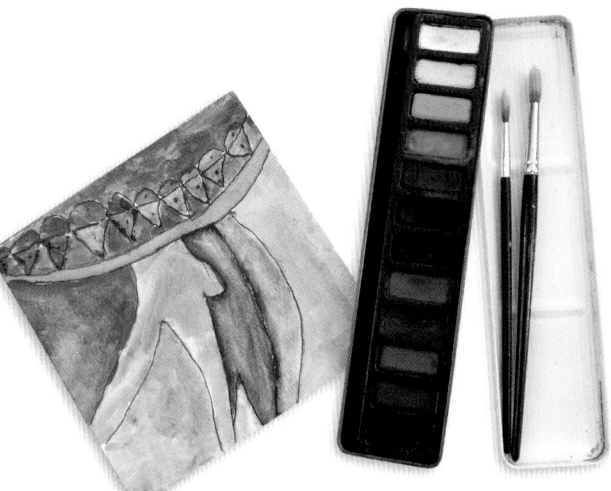

ACTIVITY

This session begins by looking at the collection of drawings that the children made in Session 3. They should each have made at least two or three, with different characteristics. Talk about the similarities and differences between them. Ask the children to comment on those they especially like and to justify their choices. Explain to the children that over the next two sessions they are going to make one small and one large painting, and that they can choose different designs for each. They will make small watercolour paintings first and then combine these later to make large-scale paintings with poster paints or coloured inks and pens.

- Encourage pupils to think carefully about the designs they choose. Suggest that they do not necessarily need to work faithfully from one or more of their own drawings but could choose aspects of other people's work too. They could work with a partner or in a group, combining parts of each others' drawings with their own.
- Distribute squares of watercolour paper and ask the children to draw a

design very lightly in soft pencil. If preferred, you could give them time to plan their idea in a box on a page of their sketchbook, before drafting it onto their watercolour square.

- When they are happy with their design, they can start to paint it, choosing the colours that they observed in the still-life arrangement and mixing varying strengths of paint. Pupils can try to match colours if they want to or simply enjoy the experience of painting little decorative pieces in colours of their choice. These small paintings should not take too long and some children will have time to make a second. Encourage the children to use different opacities of paint within each fresh square.
- When the small paintings are finished, lay them out all together on

a table or on the floor and gather the children round. Ask them to identify any that they particularly like and to give reasons for their choices. Try rearranging them in different ways or let the children take turns at altering the position of some. In the next session, pupils will be using and adapting their designs to make some large-scale paintings. After this, the paintings can be assembled together as a large square or rectangular display.

■ Bring the class together for a plenary discussion to review the children's work and suggest improvements.

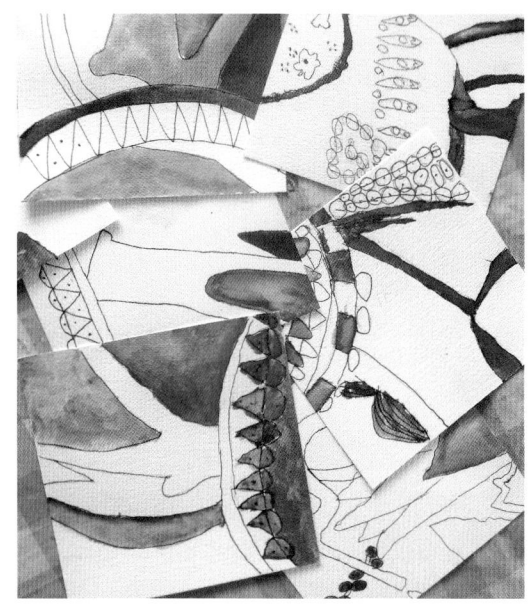

DIFFERENTIATION

Children who have not progressed as far…
Some children may struggle with the idea of exploring several ideas and making decisions about which particular compositions to take forward. They may need adult support to make these choices or could work in partnership with another child who can help them.

Children who have progressed further…
These children could be challenged to try out contrasting ideas in their paintings. For example, they could be asked to represent very different aspects of the still life in each piece of work, to use the paint in contrasting ways or to use varying kinds of paint.

SESSION 5 PAINTINGS LARGE AND SMALL 2

LEARNING OBJECTIVES

Children will:

- learn to experiment freely and confidently with approaches to painting in sketchbooks, and make personal decisions and informed choices
- increase their understanding of paint and how it can be used for different effects

- develop their critical understanding by using appropriate vocabulary to express opinions about their paintings and those of others.

VOCABULARY associated with colour and qualities of paint, such as **primary, secondary, opaque, translucent, thick, thin, warm, cool, light, dark, matt, shiny, tone, tint, shade**

▼ RESOURCES

- ▸ powder paint, poster paint or tempera blocks in the following colours: two blues (brilliant blue and cobalt blue, or cyan or turquoise); two reds (vermillion and crimson); two yellows (brilliant yellow and lemon yellow) plus black and white
- ▸ OR coloured drawing inks (these can stain so must be used with old clothing or overalls)
- ▸ a range of brushes – large and small, round and square-ended
- ▸ paint palettes for mixing
- ▸ water containers and sponges, rags or paper towels to dry brushes on
- ▸ sketchbooks
- ▸ viewfinder watercolour paintings from Session 4
- ▸ large sheets of robust white (cartridge) paper or card
- ▸ soft pencils
- ▸ bold marker pens
- ▸ resource sheet: Making your mark
- ▸ pupil self-evaluation sheet

ACTIVITY

This session is the culmination of the unit and will provide an opportunity for pupils to increase their skills in managing and controlling paint with a creative and individual response. The children will make a final painting, exploring different design ideas and consolidating their learning. For this painting they may experiment with paints or inks that they not have used before, so they will need to do some practising in their sketchbooks.

- Allow them a few minutes at the start of the session to discover how to make:
  - a strong, intense pigment (*opaque*)
  - a delicate wash (*translucent*)
  - some dots, dashes, wavy, straight, zigzag and curly lines (and any others)
  - a *secondary* colour from two *primary* colours
  - three more versions of that secondary colour, each one a different shade
  - a *warm* and a *cool* shade
  - a lighter *tone* made by adding white
  - a darker *shade* made by adding a touch of black
  - marks with both big and small brushes.
- Alternatively, reintroduce the **Making your mark** resource sheet and ask the children to revisit some of the marks that it suggests, so they have time to explore what the paint or ink

they are using can do, and how it differs from the watercolours they used in Session 4.

- Now assemble the small paintings made in Session 4 and talk to the children about how they could select elements of the patterns they painted before to create new designs. Model the process of choosing, for example,

a spiral from one pattern, some zigzags or stripes from somewhere else and combining these however they want to. Talk about big, bold designs and encourage them to think of and describe lots of examples, as they are going to work on a large scale. Although the painting would normally be considered an individual activity, it could also work well if done by children in pairs, especially where there is limited table space to work on a large scale.

■ Let them try out a few ideas initially in their sketchbooks and then draft these lightly on to large squares of paper. When they are happy with their designs, they can outline them with bold marker pens or simply start painting, with whatever combination of colours they choose. Encourage them to switch brushes for large and small areas of their paintings and to mix their own shades rather than using them as they come. Remind the children that they can use paint in different strengths, that they can make their colours darker and lighter

(shading and tinting) and that they can share colours they have mixed with a partner or with others on their table.

■ When the paintings are complete, they can be displayed all together or mounted and displayed individually. Give pupils an opportunity to make comparisons between their work and others', to talk about what they have done and the choices they made, and to describe any refinements they might like to make to their work.

■ At the end of the session, compare the children's work with that of other artists in a plenary discussion. You may also like to provide each child with the **Pupil self-evaluation** sheet for feedback on the work undertaken during this unit.

▼ ASSESSMENT FOR
LEARNING

Can the children:
▶ experiment confidently in sketchbooks and understand the concept of trying out different ideas to develop for their compositions?
▶ demonstrate increased skills and understanding in the design choices they make, the application of paint and the selection of colours?
▶ compare their own work with that of others, and reflect on and implement ways in which they might alter and improve?

DIFFERENTIATION

Children who have not progressed as far…
These pupils may need assistance in the planning and drafting stages of their paintings and could work in pairs and help one another. They may need to be reminded to explore a broad range of colours and encouraged to try paints or inks with which they are less familiar.

Children who have progressed further…
These children may feel confident playing with ideas and creating designs with more complex arrangements of shapes. They could also be challenged to be adventurous in their choice of colours and to experiment with a combination of paints.

OTHER AREAS OF LEARNING

SCIENCE

- Demonstrate how pigments are used to make up paint and ink colours. Take a piece of filter paper and wet the centre slightly. Draw a large dot in the middle with a felt-tip pen. The ink will bleed into the paper and show the different colours that make up the overall colour. Cheaper felt-tip pens work better.

MATHEMATICS

- Encourage the use of mathematical vocabulary when pupils are exploring pattern in objects and artefacts.
- Encourage the use of positional vocabulary when pupils are describing the whereabouts of objects within a still life.

HISTORY

- Pupils can research still-life paintings linked with periods being studied and explore what the content of a painting reveals about the place and time it was made.
- Pupils can make a Roman, Tudor or Ancient Greek arrangement and draw, paint or photograph it.

ART AND DESIGN

- Pupils could make collaged still lifes using a combination of painted images and photographs cut out of magazines.
- Pupils could make 3D still-life arrangements from small objects arranged in a shoe box like a stage set, photograph different versions and choose their favourite.
- Pupils can explore the meaning and significance of pattern in Islamic textiles, tiles and decoration.

Painting

PHYSICAL, SOCIAL AND HEALTH EDUCATION (PSHE)

- Looking at works of art and artefacts from other cultures can help broaden pupils' knowledge and understanding of others' customs and traditions and their respect for cultural differences.

ICT

- Use digital cameras to photograph patterned fabrics, wrapping papers and other patterned objects collected by the children. Download the photos and view on screen as a slide show or open within an image-manipulation programme and explore adaptations of scale, colour and arrangement.
- Pupils could find out more about the genre of still life and make a leaflet, booklet or *PowerPoint* presentation.

LITERACY

- Pupils can make an information booklet or zigzag book to explain about still life – what it is, what it might contain and display some well-known examples.
- Describe to pupils a still-life painting that they cannot see and ask them to draw what they visualise from your description.
- Pupils can study a collection of a dozen or more still-life images (postcards, reproductions or on the interactive whiteboard) and debate which six should be chosen for an exhibition.

By Year 3, pupils should have a basic understanding of what a print is, and that there are several ways to make one. They should be able to describe one or more of these ways, and understand that a print can be obtained by pressing objects onto inked surfaces, or vice versa. At this stage, the children are ready to experiment with other printing tools, textures and surfaces, and explore the various choices they offer.

Prior to Year 3, children will have discovered that marks can be made by pressing the finger or other objects into or onto a surface, such as a wall or sand, and that these marks can be varied according to the colour, angle, pressure and tools used. They will have learned that when marks are made in this way, by one stamp only, they are called prints, and that they differ from marks made by other mark-making methods, such as drawing or painting. They will be able to use a limited vocabulary related to printing and have the motor-control skills needed for basic pressure prints.

In this unit, pupils will be given opportunities to use a wider range of printing materials and techniques to further develop their motor-control skills, build planning and prediction skills, and use further relevant vocabulary. Alternative ways of applying colour will be introduced, encouraging children to make choices and create their own designs from stimuli. The sessions are carefully structured to utilise the skills gained in *Art Express* Books 1 and 2 to encourage pupils to find creative ways to solve printing problems and meet printing challenges, as well as providing clear instruction.

It may be worthwhile creating a classroom 'print box' containing all the print tools needed throughout the unit, rather than trying to source them as needed in individual sessions.

AIMS

This unit offers children the opportunity to:
- experiment more widely with different variables, such as shape, pressure, method, tools, materials or colour, and begin to think more creatively about the application of techniques, setting themselves standards and visual goals
- begin to be more discerning in their use of pattern and balance in colour and composition, experimenting with a wider range of tools and techniques
- understand and use appropriate and relevant vocabulary
- use planning and predicting skills, and make choices as to how they can develop or modify their own printing
- develop a recognition and a greater awareness of print in their own environment and culture, and of printing in other cultures, countries and periods of history.

ASSESSMENT FOR LEARNING

Assessment is ongoing throughout the unit, with specific questions suggested during the sessions, such as: *Can the children say what makes the inks float?* This is in addition to challenges and problem-solving activities to produce evidence of specific skills and thought processes, such as: *Challenge the children to come up with a way of achieving a more accurate print.* Suggested questions for assessment are also given at the end of each session and on the resource sheets.

▶ CD-ROM RESOURCES
- Artworks and images
- Resource sheets:
  - Plaster cast prints
  - Marbling
  - Pounced stencil prints
- Teacher assessment
- Pupil self-evaluation

SESSION | **PLASTER-CAST PRINTS**

LEARNING OBJECTIVES
Children will:
■ learn a further application of printing by making an impression of an object in clay
■ extend their understanding of different materials by comparing them and observing how they work together

■ develop a recognition that many objects used all over the world are made using impressions and moulds.

VOCABULARY **imprint, impression, cast, mould**

▼ RESOURCES

▸ moulded objects, such as plastic or rubber toy, candle, chocolate bar, ice cube, metal medal (some examples on the CD-ROM)
▸ modelling/natural clay
▸ selection of sweets with distinctive shapes; small shells
▸ jug and spoon
▸ plaster of Paris
▸ margarine or ice-cream tub
▸ paints and brushes
▸ CD-ROM: images of footprints
▸ resource sheet: Plaster-cast prints

ACTIVITY

Show the class the moulded objects, ask what they have in common and discuss how they have been made. They all involve pouring a liquid into a *mould*. The liquid takes on the exact shape of the mould. Ask pupils if any liquid would do. Can they work out that it needs to be a liquid that is capable of hardening? Discuss what would happen if water were poured into a mould. What would they have to do to it to make a moulded object? (It would have to be frozen so that it hardened into ice.) The details of the mould *imprint* themselves onto the liquid as it hardens. What other moulded objects can they think of or see in the classroom? Show the CD-ROM images of footprints. These have been imprinted into the sand by pressure. The feet have left moulds or *impressions*. If someone poured a liquid into these moulds and allowed it to harden, they could make a cast of the footprints. (Pupils may know that police detectives use this method for tracking down criminals who have left shoe prints at a crime scene.)

■ Roll out the clay into a thick slab. Natural clay is much better than self-hardening clay as it contains no fibres and therefore produces a much cleaner and more accurate result (and is much cheaper!). Show pupils how to push the

▸ INFORMATION
You can re-use the clay for modelling, but do not kiln-fire clay that has been used for plasterwork, as even small traces of plaster can cause models to crack or explode in the kiln.

sweets and shells, with the top surface facing downwards, into the clay and remove them carefully to leave a clear, deep print, like the footprints on the CD-ROM. Challenge them to work out how they can avoid wasting sweets (by using the same sweet several times). They should now refer to this as their *impression* or *mould*.

■ Pour a few centimetres of water into the jug. Gradually add plaster of Paris until the mound protrudes from the water. Stir until a thickish liquid is formed. Immediately pour or spoon the liquid into the clay impressions or moulds and leave to set. Splashes and drips can be broken off later. Note that wet plaster gives off heat, although it is quite safe for pupils to pour. (Remember: Always pour plaster into water; never water into the plaster. This is a good opportunity for links with science – see Other Areas of Learning, page 46.)

■ Mix more plaster as needed. Challenge pupils to explain why any spare plaster should be poured straight away into the ice-cream tub to harden and be disposed of later – and why spare plaster should not be poured down the sink or drain!

■ Leave the plaster impressions to dry thoroughly, then remove them from

the clay. The hard shapes are called *casts*. Pupils may paint them if they wish. Once the technique is mastered, the children can make casts for a class project, such as a chess set or gingerbread house (see photographs).

■ **The Plaster-cast prints** resource sheet can be used after the session to revisit and consolidate the work.

▼ ASSESSMENT FOR LEARNING

Can the children:

▶ describe how they made a three-dimensional copy of an object by printing it in clay?

▶ talk about the differences between the materials they have used and say how they affect each other?

▶ give examples of moulded objects that are made and used around the world?

DIFFERENTIATION

Children who have not progressed as far...
If children find manipulating small objects difficult, encourage them to push their fingertips into the clay instead of sweets or shells, and make plaster impressions of these instead.

Children who have progressed further...
Ask these pupils to suggest and try other suitable objects to make impressions. Challenge them to think of ways to use the sweet and shell impressions for extended projects (see Other Areas of Learning, page 46, for ideas).

SESSION 2 **FOLDED MONOPRINTS**

LEARNING OBJECTIVES

Children will:

- learn to experiment creatively by making monoprints from paint pressed between two layers of paper
- learn to plan and predict how the paint will behave on the paper when pressed

- develop practical skills by creating a detailed and accurate image from a stimulus using close observation, and mixed printing tools and methods.

VOCABULARY monoprint, symmetrical, accurate, background, foreground, landscape, portrait, neutral

▼ RESOURCES

- ▸ photographs of insects
- ▸ A2 paper in neutral colours (these complement the images much better than bright colours)
- ▸ liquid paints and brushes
- ▸ range of printing tools (sponges, pencils, stiff card pieces and so on)
- ▸ metallic paints, pastels, crayons, sequins, beads for finishing touches
- ▸ CD-ROM: images of insects

ACTIVITY

Gather the class where they can see the CD-ROM images. Ask, *Apart from being insects, what do they have in common?* They are symmetrical – one side of their body matches the other side. Can pupils point out any other symmetrical objects or images in the classroom? Can they suggest how a symmetrical print might be made? They have probably made symmetrical 'butterfly' prints by placing blobs of paint on one side of a piece of paper, folding it in half and peeling it open. Invite a child to demonstrate this. It is called a *monoprint* because it is a single

print, made in a single movement. Can pupils think of other words that use the prefix *mono-*? The class could discuss the prefix and its meaning.

- Seat the children in preparation to make their prints. Is the monoprint they just made an *accurate* representation of a butterfly? Can the children say what could be done to improve it? They might suggest close observation of the shapes and patterns of the butterfly, or careful colour mixing. Challenge them to decide how the paint could be applied so that the print would be more accurate. They will need to consider the position of the paint and the amount applied. Ask, *Would it be wiser to apply a little or a lot of paint at once?* Would the children start with light or dark colours, large or small areas, background or foreground colours?

- Provide pupils with photographs of insects (one each, or placed where they can clearly see one). Ask each child to study their insect closely and decide whether to have their paper landscape or portrait to fit the shape of their insect before folding their paper in half vertically. Invite them to plan how to begin their print, perhaps by mixing the main background colour of their insect as accurately as possible and applying the colour to one half of the paper. Remind pupils that when the paper is squashed together, the colour

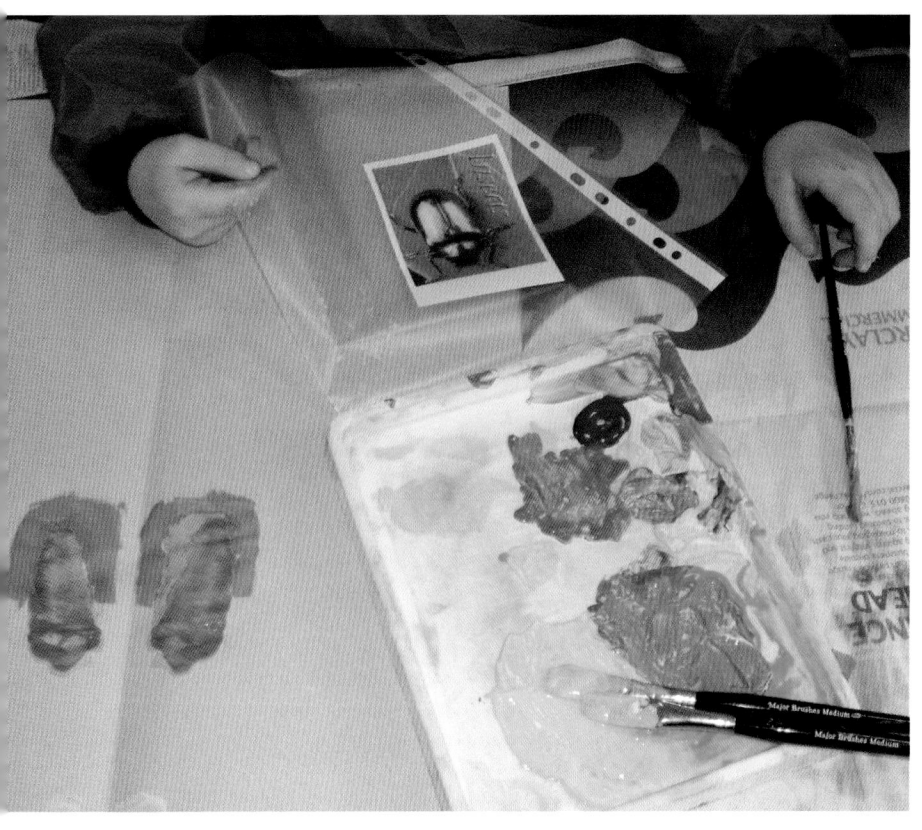

will spread. They should then fold together and peel open, and plan the next stage having seen the result. Encourage finding ways to incorporate, disguise or improve mistakes, rather than starting again.

■ Pupils should gradually build up further areas of the insect. Do they think a brush is always the best tool to apply the paint? If not, they can try other items, such as fingers, sponges or vegetable pieces. Each time fresh paint is applied, they should press the paper in half before the paint dries.

■ Children can add tiny details such as hairs or antennae by printing onto both sides of the opened-out monoprint using smaller tools. Encourage them to choose suitable tools for certain effects, such as string, edges of card or ends of pencils.

■ If they wish, they can add other finishing touches to the prints, such as metallic paints, pastels or crayons, sequins or beads. Encourage them to keep such additions subtle, to echo the

real appearance of the insect, rather than over-using them purely as decoration.

■ In a plenary discussion, encourage pupils to discuss their work and what they have made and to make an evaluation of their own work.

▼ ASSESSMENT FOR LEARNING

Can the children:
▶ describe the print they have made and how they made it, using relevant vocabulary?
▶ choose suitable tools to print smaller details on their insect and say why they chose them?
▶ predict how the amount and position of paint, and the order in which they apply it to the paper, will affect the end result?

DIFFERENTIATION

Children who have not progressed as far...
These pupils can experiment freely with blobs of paint, discovering how far it spreads, how much or little to use, how colours mingle together, and how long it needs to dry before another colour can be applied.

Children who have progressed further...
Set further folded monoprint challenges for these children, such as a symmetrical flying bird printed entirely with the fingers, or a detailed tropical fish printed only with vegetables.
See also the Mathematics section of Other Areas of Learning, page 46.

SESSION 3 MARBLING ON PAPER

LEARNING OBJECTIVES
Children will:
- develop practical skills by creating a print on paper from inks floating on water
- further develop their ability to experiment creatively by suggesting and exploring ways in which the results can be used
- learn to recognise and describe the properties of materials by working with inks, reflecting on how they float, drip and constantly change due to movement.

VOCABULARY marbling, surface, absorb, evaporate; adjectives and similes to describe the appearance of the marbling: **glossy, movable, mobile, sliding, shiny, matt, dull**

▼ RESOURCES

- ▶ develop practical skills by creating a print on paper from inks floating on water
- ▶ further develop their ability to experiment creatively by suggesting and exploring ways in which the results can be used
- ▶ learn to recognise and describe the properties of materials by working with inks, reflecting on how they float, drip and constantly change due to movement
- ▶ CD-ROM: images of marble objects and real marble

▼ ASSESSMENT FOR LEARNING

Can the children:
- ▶ describe the patterns on their print and say whether they remind them of anything?
- ▶ explain why no two prints will be the same?
- ▶ say why it is important that the inks float?

ACTIVITY

Show the CD-ROM images of real marble and marble objects. Demonstrate the marbling method: drop two or three drops of the marbling ink onto the surface of the water, using no more than two colours. Ask a child to gently pull the inks into swirls on the water using a cocktail stick or skewer. When a pleasing pattern is achieved, hold a sheet of paper by one corner and carefully lower it onto the surface to take a print. Let go of the corner to avoid leaving a plain patch. Lift out straight away and ask pupils why the marbling should be dried horizontally. (If hung, the pattern will run downwards.)
- After this initial demonstration, the marbling is best done with one or two children at a time. The rest of the class can be making small books, for which the marbling can be used as covers, or assembling materials for an underwater collage, for which the marbling can provide a background. The marbling requires drying time before it can be used.
- Ask, *What are the differences between the marbling on the paper when it was still wet, and the marbling when it is dry?* Encourage descriptive vocabulary such as *glossy, movable* or *mobile, sliding, shiny, matt,* and factual accuracy, such as, *The inks are absorbed by the paper,* or, *As the water evaporates, the ink and paper turn dull.* Make a list of the descriptive words and encourage pupils to use them throughout the unit.
- Can they say why the inks float, and how a print might be taken? Could you obtain two identical prints?
- A second, more delicate print can be taken before adding more ink. Do not allow too much ink, or too many colours, to build up on the water. Ask pupils how unwanted ink can be removed. (By taking more prints!)

DIFFERENTIATION

Children who have not progressed as far...
Marbling is usually achievable by all ability levels, but if pupils find the book-making or the cutting involved in collage difficult, invite them to find ways to print sea creatures on their marbled paper using a variety of objects and methods they have explored before.

Children who have progressed further...
Challenge these children to work out a way of taking a different marbling print on different areas of paper, by dipping only certain sections or folding the paper. They could also experiment with overlapping prints.

SESSION 4 MARBLING ON CLOTH

LEARNING OBJECTIVES

Children will:

- reaffirm their capacity to experiment creatively with marbling on further surfaces
- extend practical skills learned in the previous session by creating a print on cloth using floating inks
- learn to plan, improve and modify their design by embellishing their print with stitching or further printing.

VOCABULARY **cloth** (this word is more accurate than *material* or *fabric*, which have other meanings)

ACTIVITY

Look with the class at the marbled paper made in Session 3. Revisit the descriptions of the differences between the wet and the dry marbling, checking that pupils understand that the water is absorbed by the paper and gradually evaporates. Show pupils the plain cloth and ask whether it could be marbled and, if so, how. For example, if the cloth were large, you could dip a section at a time to make a sea drape, or you could print small individual pieces. As a class, decide what you would like to do.

■ Follow the instructions for Session 3, using the cloth instead of paper. Ask pupils to predict what differences there will be between marbling paper and marbling the cloth, and whether they think the cloth can be dried vertically (unlike the paper) and, if so, why.

■ When dry, the marbled cloth can be embellished with stitching, sequins or beads. You can also place a layer of quilting beneath the cloth, and a smooth, thin piece of fabric beneath the quilting, and stitch through all three layers to produce a cushioned or 3D effect. (See also Differentiation.)

■ Ask pupils to suggest other surfaces that could be marbled – for example, plain white objects, such as the cut-off lower half of washing-up liquid bottles (sandpapered to remove lettering) or paper plates.

■ Experiment with printing on alternative objects and surfaces – sandpaper, clingfilm, tin foil – and ask pupils to describe the results, verbally or in writing.

■ The **Marbling** resource sheet can be used to revisit and consolidate the work covered in Sessions 3 and 4.

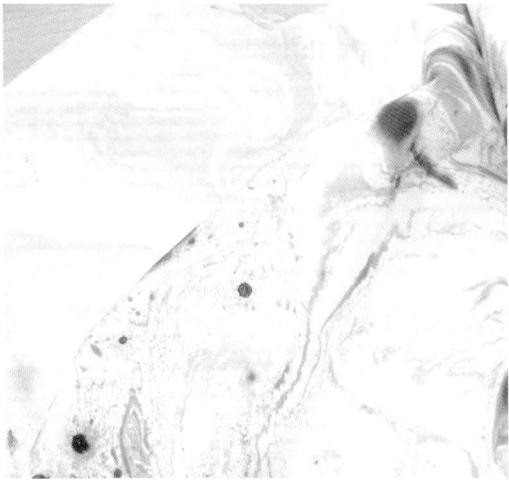

RESOURCES

▶ as for Session 3, but substitute the paper with plain cloth with some cotton content (as cloth is more absorbent, it can be hung to dry vertically)
▶ needles, threads, scissors, sequins, beads for embellishment
▶ resource sheet: Marbling

ASSESSMENT FOR LEARNING

Can the children:

▶ explain how cloth differs from paper and how this affects the print?
▶ describe what their print looks like and find appropriate ways to embellish it?
▶ discuss together and reach decisions about what experiments to carry out?

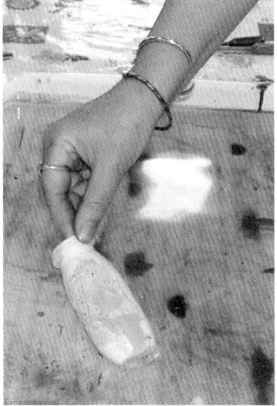

DIFFERENTIATION

Children who have not progressed as far…
If stitching is too difficult, further printing can be added with small tools. Ask the children to suggest what their print reminds them of, such as a sea bed or the surface of a planet, to help them decide what to add. They could make a list of descriptive words to explain their work.

Children who have progressed further…
Challenge these pupils to design and make an item using marbled cloth. Ask them to consider whether it is wiser to marble the cloth first and then construct the item, or the other way around, and give reasons for their decision.

SESSION 5 **POUNCED STENCIL PRINTS**

LEARNING OBJECTIVES

Children will:

- reaffirm their confidence and capacity to experiment creatively by developing compositions from shapes based on architecture
- extend practical skills by making and using a pounce and cutting stencils
- develop critical understanding by exploring what is meant by positive and negative images.

VOCABULARY stencil, angular, architecture, negative/positive image or shape, composition, structure, rigid, pounce, dolly, apply, technique, method; **shape-related words: rhombus, trapezium, parallelogram, rectangle, square, oblong, pentagon, hexagon, octagon, triangle, isosceles, equilateral, acute, obtuse, right-angled**

▼ RESOURCES

- ▶ pencils, rulers and scissors
- ▶ scrap paper
- ▶ old clean socks and soft pieces of rag
- ▶ printing trays, rollers and printing inks
- ▶ background paper
- ▶ CD-ROM: images of angles, straight lines and edges in architecture from around the world
- ▶ resource sheet: Pounced stencil prints

ACTIVITY

Look at the architectural images on the CD-ROM. Discuss what shapes pupils can find in the buildings and invite the children to choose suitable adjectives to describe them. What are the main shapes the architect has used in the classroom or school? Ask the children why they think angular shapes are often used in architecture. They are often used to create a *rigid structure*. If you wish, introduce some of the shape-related words in Vocabulary (see also the **Pounced stencil prints** resource sheet).

- Ask pupils to use pencils and rulers

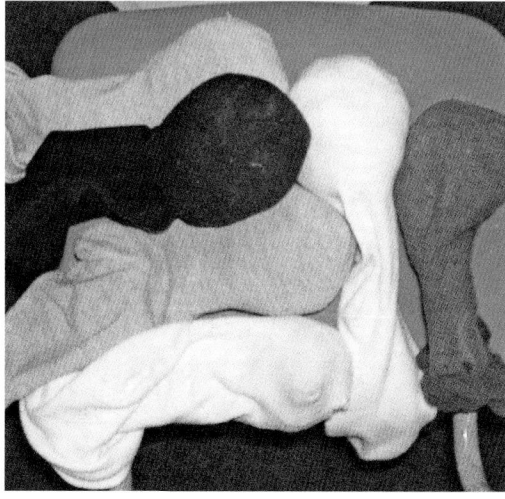

to design angular shapes on the paper and cut them out. Ask, *In what ways could we use these shapes to make a print?* They could ink the shape and press it onto paper, or print around its edge. Invite the children to suggest suitable tools or methods for this – for example, a sponge or fingers.

- Take a sock and ask if this would be a good tool! Stuff the end with a soft rag until the toe section is round. This is called a *pounce* or *dolly*. It is a good tool for inking stencils, awkward areas or uneven surfaces.
- Roll some ink thinly on a tray. Pick up some ink on the pounce and invite a child to press and slightly roll it, gently and evenly, around the shape onto the background paper. Remove the stencil. This is called a negative image. Does the texture of the sock affect the print? Ask pupils to make their own pounces. Provide four or

five trays of ink, each with a different colour. Trays can be moved around the groups, or children can visit different tables to use a variety of ink colours.

■ Using the images of architecture as inspiration, pupils should experiment with placing the cut-out shapes on their background paper, and then use the pounce around their edges to make negative prints. Encourage them to take ideas from the architectural images to make a balanced abstract composition, rather than constructing a symbol of a house or building.

■ Next, challenge pupils to find a way to cut out more shapes without cutting in from the edge of the paper. Demonstrate that rather than trying to poke the scissors through the middle of the shape, they can pinch the paper into a fold in the centre of the shape and snip through it.

■ Show the piece of paper from which you cut the shape. Ask, *In what ways could we use this to make a print?* They could roll the whole piece with ink and press it on to another sheet of paper.

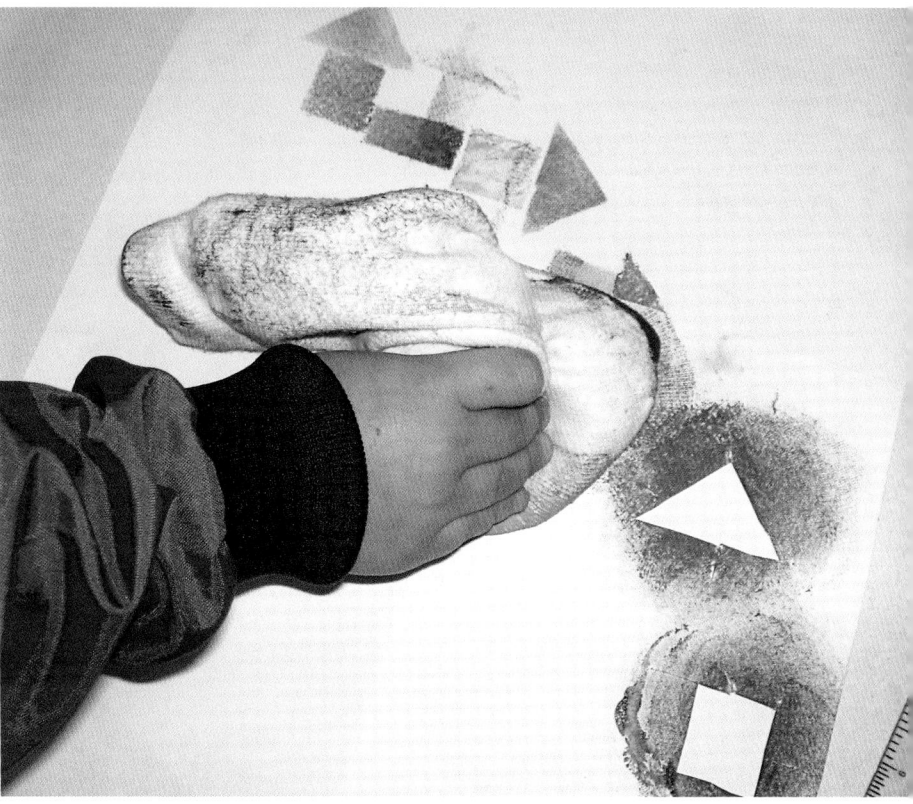

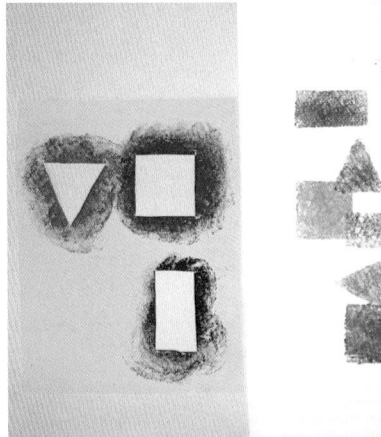

Ask, *Would this give a positive or negative image? How could we print a positive image using the paper?* Can pupils work out that they would have to put the piece of paper over a background piece and use the pounce to apply ink through the hole?

■ Invite children to add positive images to their design. Pupils can save their inked cut-out shapes, and use them when dry to add to their print or to make a collage of positive shapes.

■ The **Pounced stencil prints** resource sheet can be used to consolidate the work covered in this session.

▼ ASSESSMENT FOR LEARNING

Can the children:
▸ show evidence of using the ideas in the architecture to inspire their design?
▸ explain how they made the pounce and find a way to cut shapes from the middle of the paper and not from the edge?
▸ explain or point out examples of positive and negative images?

DIFFERENTIATION

Children who have not progressed as far...
These children may need to have the shapes cut out by an adult. Set simpler challenges, such as printing a row of triangles to resemble roofs.

Children who have progressed further...
These pupils can experiment with further shapes cut from within, or use different pounce textures and pressures. Set challenges, such as printing rows of houses or hills that are paler in the distance and get darker as they reach the foreground. You could also ask them to write definitions of some of the mathematical terms to share with the class.

SESSION 6 **PRINTING CHALLENGE**

LEARNING OBJECTIVES

Children will:

- extend practical skills by creating a composite print using a range of tools and methods
- develop their capacity as independent learners by building on existing experience to make choices about design and composition
- learn to discuss, experiment with and take inspiration from a variety of stimuli.

VOCABULARY See Sessions 1–5

▼ RESOURCES

- ▶ wide range of materials and objects, such as fruit bags, cloth, corrugated card, net, foil, boxes, plastic toys, sticks, cotton reels, lipstick tops, tubes
- ▶ trays, inks and rollers
- ▶ sponges
- ▶ bottled paints
- ▶ pounces
- ▶ scrap paper
- ▶ A2 background paper
- ▶ CD-ROM: images of vehicles and sea creatures
- ▶ pupil self-evaluation sheet

ACTIVITY

Talk about and, if possible, look at previous examples of printing you have done. Invite pupils to recall and explain how they made the prints and what tools and methods they used. Explain that they are now going to be given a choice of printing methods, materials and tools, and two choices of printing challenge. They must choose a challenge and decide which methods and tools are suitable for meeting it.

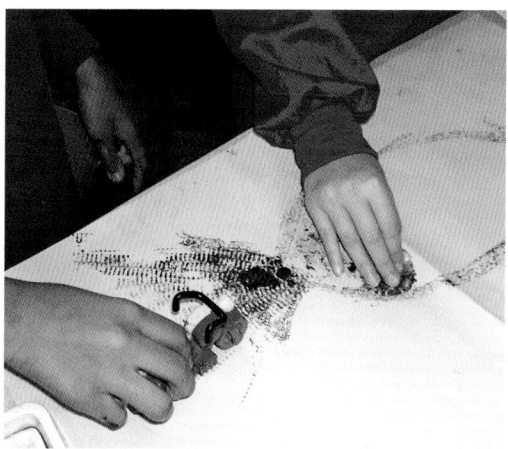

■ Show the range of tools and materials you have gathered. (These should not necessarily be specifically chosen to make 'good' prints – rather, provide a box of whatever items you happen to have, so children are encouraged to look at their creative possibilities and printing potential.) Show the choice of printing methods – paint on a tray, paint on a sponge on a tray, inks and rollers, inks and pounces. Point out that some methods suit certain objects better than others – for example, you could ink the end of a tube efficiently with a pounce, but not very efficiently with a roller.

■ Show the class the **CD-ROM** images of vehicles and sea creatures. Their choice of challenge is to print any vehicle or sea creature, either directly from the images or based on them.

■ Pupils should now move to their work areas and begin planning their print. Once they have chosen the subject of their challenge, they should choose their background paper and decide whether to place it in the portrait or landscape position. Throughout the session, use and reinforce the vocabulary introduced in previous sessions, and give the children opportunities to use it.

■ Suggest that pupils do not print directly onto their background paper, but first try out some methods and tools on scrap paper until they have

a bank of ideas to draw on. As pupils build up their 'print-bank', encourage and give praise for experimenting with one tool and a range of methods, or one method and a range of tools, exhausting all possibilities and choosing the most effective, rather than flitting from one idea to another. Show examples of interesting results to the class and encourage sharing ideas rather than guarding them.

■ When they have built up a reasonable print-bank, pupils will need to plan their composition. Remind them that once a print is placed on the paper it cannot be undone, so car wheels and sea creatures' heads must be placed accurately first time around, leaving room for the rest of the design.

■ Ask the children to use their previous knowledge to make decisions about colour. Is it wise to start with black

and, if not, why not? Reinforce the wisdom of building up gradually from pale to dark colours.

■ Pupils can now use the ideas from their print-bank to build their design. If things go wrong, encourage them to find ways of using mistakes positively – for example, an unintentional mark on a sea creature can be repeated all over it to become a pattern. Rather than providing them with new paper, the children can print over mistakes, or glue other printed paper over them to form a printed collage.

■ At the end of the session, provide each child with the **Pupil self-evaluation** sheet for feedback on the work undertaken in the unit.

▼ ASSESSMENT FOR LEARNING

Can the children:
▶ show evidence of planning and select appropriate tools and methods to carry this out?
▶ talk about and give reasons for the choices they have made about their design?
▶ show evidence of using previous experience and ideas from the stimuli offered?

DIFFERENTIATION

Children who have not progressed as far…
Restrict the range of tools and methods offered, and encourage full exploration of each tool until these pupils build more confidence. Rather than giving ideas, ask them to see what marks each tool prints on scrap paper and what ideas these suggest to them.

Children who have progressed further…
Offer further challenges to these children, such as printing suitable backgrounds or adding details to the print, such as individual scales, tyre tracks or shadows.

OTHER AREAS OF LEARNING

ART AND DESIGN

- Design a Gingerbread Cottage (from the fairy tale *Hansel and Gretel*) or a chess set using plaster-cast sweets (see photographs, Session 1). Pupils need to consider size, shape, colour and relationships between these when designing.

LITERACY

- Explore phrases based on printing, such as: *imprinted on my memory*, *made a lasting impression on me*, *cast in the same mould* and *printed on my brain*.
- Use the marbling patterns created in Sessions 3 and 4 to inspire descriptive writing, exploring suitable adjectives and underwater themes. Display written work on a marbled background.

DANCE

- Printing is full of movement and repetition that can be used to build a printing dance.
- The sounds associated with printing can be used to create a composition to accompany the dance.

Printing

SCIENCE

- Session 1 offers opportunities to compare materials and how they behave. What happens to the plaster when it is poured into the water? What happens when water is poured onto plaster? How does the clay affect the plaster when it is poured in? Which dries first, clay or plaster? How does water affect clay? Try taking prints in dry, semi-dry, moist or over-wet clay.
- Sessions 3 and 4 offer opportunities to experiment with floating and sinking.

MATHEMATICS

- The sweets and shells made in Session 1 can be used to support maths and money activities. Ask pupils to design a sweet or seaside shop or stall in the classroom and to price each item.
- Links with symmetry, pattern and balance are offered in Session 2. Pupils can try working out ways to print objects that have more than one line of symmetry, such as snowflakes.
- The theme for Session 6 can lead to work on angles, shape and measurement, particularly on types of triangle.

HISTORY

- Session 1 deals with impressions, imprints, casts and moulds, of which there are many ancient examples. Explain that the study of dinosaur and human footprints can tell us the size and weight of the creatures that made them. Show images of moulds and casts from different cultures, including Ancient Egypt and Ancient Greece.
- The history of printing itself is a vast and fascinating topic – books, cloth and patterning of all kinds show evidence that humans have used the technique since very early times.

Materials are all around us – the clothes we wear and love, alongside the paper we draw on, both form part of our everyday life. Collage or mixed media (the assemblage of materials and images to create new ones) and textiles (any kind of woven, knitted, hand-made, machine-made or non-woven fabric) both supplement each other in the classroom. Exciting and inspiring first-hand source materials bring the visual and tactile together in and outside the classroom, and make learning about new processes and techniques more accessible and real.

Prior to Year 3, early playful experience of collage and textiles will have included exploring materials, their uses and properties, and investigating a wide range of materials, fabrics, threads and papers. Weaving in some form will have helped to reinforce how woven fabric is made and used. Sketchbooks to record explorations will have been introduced. Pupils may also have been shown the work of artists and craftspeople to gain inspiration and to learn how different cultures use and alter fabric for different purposes.

In this unit, pupils are encouraged to experiment with textiles and collage in greater depth, through drawing, dyeing, bonding, stitching, embellishing and painting. First-hand observation is a key focus – not only does it inspire, teach and inform, it also marries the tactile and the visual. Rather than just making images as part of play, images are now more carefully planned and sustained. Children need to be given free access to their sketchbooks to record ideas and sketch from life. The making of textiles is an ancient craft and is steeped in history, tradition, folklore, religious ritual and technological advances, and it is important to discuss and explore these with the class.

AIMS
This unit offers children the opportunity to:
- develop ideas and explore different starting points for collage and textile work, using a variety of methods to collect visual stimuli
- investigate different materials, changing their surface, structure and appearance using a range of techniques, and create collages
- use an extended vocabulary to describe the visual and tactile qualities of textiles, with reference to woven, stitched and dyed textiles
- compare and comment on the work of artists and craftspeople from a range of cultures and periods.

ASSESSMENT FOR LEARNING
In this unit, ongoing assessment should incorporate a wide range of recording, using photos, samples, sketches and presentations. Pupils will widen their understanding of where fabrics, patterns and designs originate and look to local crafts and other cultures to make these connections. First-hand experience of museums and galleries, embroidery, felt-making, tie and dye and collage work will reinforce this. Throughout, promote reference to artists and craftspeople. Encourage pupils to discuss possible improvement to their own and others' work to build confidence and communication skills. Overall, investigation and exploration should be fun and informative.

> ▶ **CD-ROM RESOURCES**
> Presentation: Making felt Masterclass
> Artworks and images
> Resource sheets:
>   Visiting a museum or gallery
>   Tie and dye
>   Stitching
>   Indian textile designs
>   Butterflies
> Teacher assessment
> Pupil self-evaluation

SESSION 1 GAINING INSPIRATION

----LEARNING OBJECTIVES

Children will:

- learn to generate ideas and to compare and comment on different starting points by collecting first-hand drawings, notes and images in a sketchbook
- develop their capacity as independent learners by discussing their findings and sharing ideas
- learn about the differences between different cultures, by exploring costume, fabrics and materials from different cultures and traditions.

VOCABULARY **museum, gallery, collection, investigation, curator, exhibit, display cabinets**

▼ RESOURCES

- ▸ sketchbooks (one per child)
- ▸ dry drawing materials (depending on what your venue allows – check in advance)
- ▸ CD-ROM: images of costumes, fabrics and textile manufacture
- ▸ resource sheet: Visiting a museum or gallery

ACTIVITY

The aim of this session is to use a visit as a source of inspiration, finding out about local textiles, costumes or collections and the importance they played in the past or today. Ideally, the session should take place during or after a visit to your local museum or gallery. (You could also try venues in your local community, such as a place of worship, an old property, factory, warehouse, stately home, or theatre with a costume department. If a visit is not possible, use the images of fabrics

and costumes on the CD-ROM.) It is important that you visit the museum or gallery in advance, so that you can plan your time effectively and adapt this session to fit what you find. The focus of this session is to look at local crafts, so spend time seeing what is on your doorstep, and investigate fabrics and costumes that are specific to your local collection or area.

- During your exploratory visit, plan what you want pupils to investigate – use some of the questions on the **Visiting a museum or gallery** resource sheet as a guide. Avoid tick-sheets supplied by the venue – focus on each child investigating for themselves from a few key questions stuck into their sketchbooks.
- In advance of the visit, discuss and investigate with the children what your local area was or is famous for. Ask them what local customs they know about and what costumes were or are worn. Examples might include: Morris men, uniforms, folk dance, maypole dancing, traditional costumes for celebrations or ceremonies such as Chinese New Year, religious robes, weddings, dances, or the theatre.
- The visit might include a talk or tour in the museum about local traditional textile crafts, local costume or the costumes in the collection. This could be followed by time for small groups of pupils to investigate areas you have

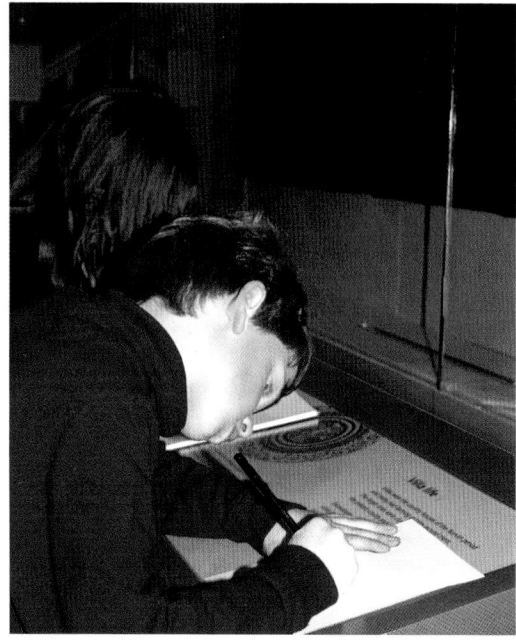

draw diagrams and find out more about the culture, traditions and period, in preparation for a short presentation. Extension work could include designing, for example, a new local costume, lace, a wall hanging or a wedding gown.

■ Ask each child or pair to present the findings of their personal study to the rest of the class. You can use this material to fuel discussions throughout the unit, making references, where possible, to the costumes and techniques observed on your visit.

▼ ASSESSMENT FOR
   LEARNING

Can the children:
▸ collect and use images and ideas in a sketchbook as inspiration for work in the classroom?
▸ begin to recognise the importance of collecting first-hand experiences?
▸ talk about the importance that costume plays in different cultures and traditions?

identified as being rich in source material. Give pupils time to collect sketches, text and annotations about aspects of the focus that interest them, such as looms, costumes, fabrics or equipment. Encourage them to make a detailed study of one item and record as much information as possible. If it is suitable or if artefacts are limited, this could be done in pairs, making sure that both parties do equal amounts of recording. If the venue will permit it, record images using a digital camera, either in advance or with the children.

■ Back in the classroom, encourage all pupils to make a personal study (perhaps using cross-curricular time, as this has local history, geography and literacy elements), finding out more about their item from the collection. They should carry out research in books and on the internet,

DIFFERENTIATION

Children who have not progressed as far...
Simplify the task in the museum, giving these pupils one or two key questions to investigate at a time. Allow them to record observations depending on their strengths – either pictorially or verbally (with a tape recorder). An adult could work with them in a small group.

Children who have progressed further...
In the museum, encourage these children to make more complex and sophisticated connections, ask more extensive questions and collate more detailed observations in note and drawing form. In the classroom, encourage them to prepare in-depth analysis of their object, making connections to local history.

SESSION 2 **TIE AND DYE**

LEARNING OBJECTIVES

Children will:

- learn to experiment and develop creativity by investigating different materials, techniques and processes

- start to understand the techniques used in dyed textiles, compare natural and synthetic dyes, and learn to be safe when dyeing
- learn about other cultures by considering how fabric is made and used.

VOCABULARY tie and dye, natural, synthetic, vat, dye, bunching, West Africa, stones, dip, soak, resist, tie, cotton

▼ RESOURCES

- ▸ a range of different fabrics or clothes that have been dyed (including tie and dye, if possible)
- ▸ 100% cotton calico or sheeting (small piece for each child)
- ▸ string, stones and sticks
- ▸ synthetic dye – Brusho, batik dye or fabric dye (from educational suppliers or fabric shops; if you are not intending to wear the item, it does not need be colourfast – refer to manufacturer's instructions)
- ▸ buckets
- ▸ tongs, rubber gloves, clothes line
- ▸ digital camera (optional)
- ▸ CD-ROM: images of tie and dye from around the world; examples of dyed fabric
- ▸ resource sheet: Tie and dye

> **! HEALTH & SAFETY**
>
> Do not allow pupils to mix the dye or put their hands into it – use a stick to push the fabric into the dye. Leave according to the manufacturer's instructions, remove (adults only) wearing rubber gloves, rinse with cold water and leave to dry.

ACTIVITY

Traditional tie-and-dye textiles are found in Latin America, the Middle East, Africa and Asia and, in the 1960s, the hippies of San Francisco, USA, also made them fashionable. Tie and dye is the simplest dye-resist technique and one of the most primitive. It is difficult to control the dye on the fabric and select the areas it fills. If twine (string or threads) is wrapped tightly around a bunch or area of fabric before it is added to a vat of dye, the areas that are covered up will resist the dye being penetrated into the surface and retain the original colour of the fabric. Bunching the fabric at intervals will give concentric circles, and rings can be formed by creating a series of wraps around the fabric (see the **Tie and dye** resource sheet for images).

■ Discuss with pupils the range of different techniques from different cultures (see the images on the CD-ROM). Talk about the meanings of *tie and dye*, *synthetic* and *natural*.

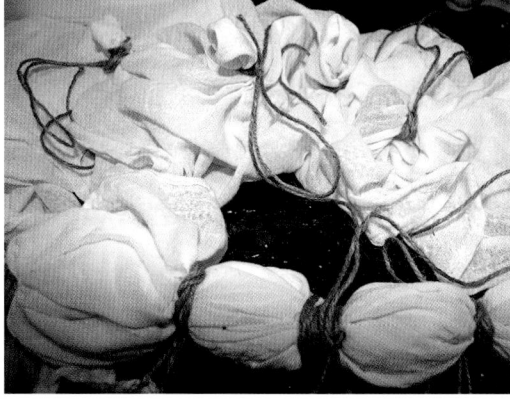

If possible, relate back to costumes or fabrics from Session 1 or use images from the CD-ROM to recap on natural dyes (see *Art Express* Book 2).

■ Demonstrate the different ways that tie and dye can be achieved, and show pupils the samples of tie-dyed fabric. Can they match the images on the **Tie and dye** resource sheet to the different techniques seen or discussed?

■ Give each child a piece of cotton fabric and ask them to experiment – they can use stones and sticks, bunch it in different places, wrap string around it or use rubber bands. Write each

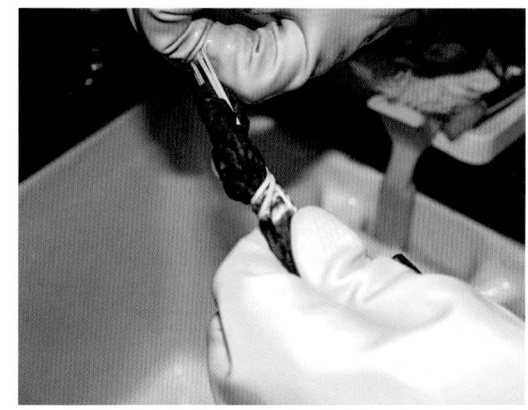

child's name on their fabric using a permanent pen before you start – once dyed, it is hard to tell! The fun of this activity is to experiment with creating different patterns on the fabric. Explain that they are trying to block the dye from impregnating the fabric, leaving those parts in the original fabric colour.

■ Break up the session, so all the tying and discussion takes place first and at the end the children select a colour to dye their work. (Have a selection of colours made up in advance.)

■ Explore fabrics and how they take colour. Use leftover dye to experiment with man-made fabric, such as polyester. Does it dye well? Experiment with pieces of cotton fabric and the length of time in the dye. Does this affect the outcome?

■ If possible, record the type of bunching and wrapping through photos or drawings before you unwrap the pieces of fabric. They can be unwrapped when they are dry (this will probably be during the next

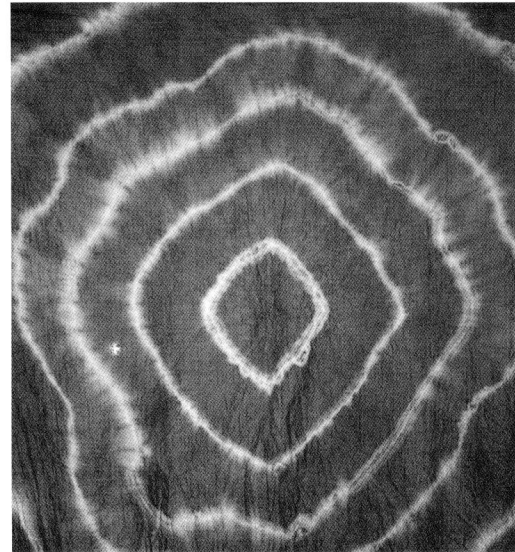

lesson). Before and after unwrapping, discuss with the class: *Which types of wrapping gave the most even effect? Which colour dye was the most effective? Look at the fabrics and try to work out how others in the class have created their designs. Did they use stones? How many bunches of string did they use?*

■ As an extension, pupils can embellish their work by adding buttons, sequins or stitches after learning about stitching in Session 3.

ASSESSMENT FOR LEARNING

Can the children:
▶ experiment purposefully with different techniques for tying and bunching the fabric?
▶ describe how to be safe when using dye?
▶ recognise dyed fabric and the process of tie-dyeing used in other cultures and describe the sequence?

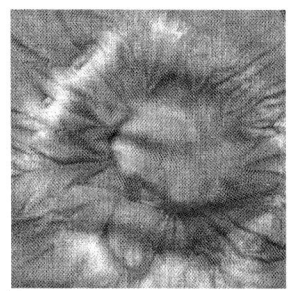

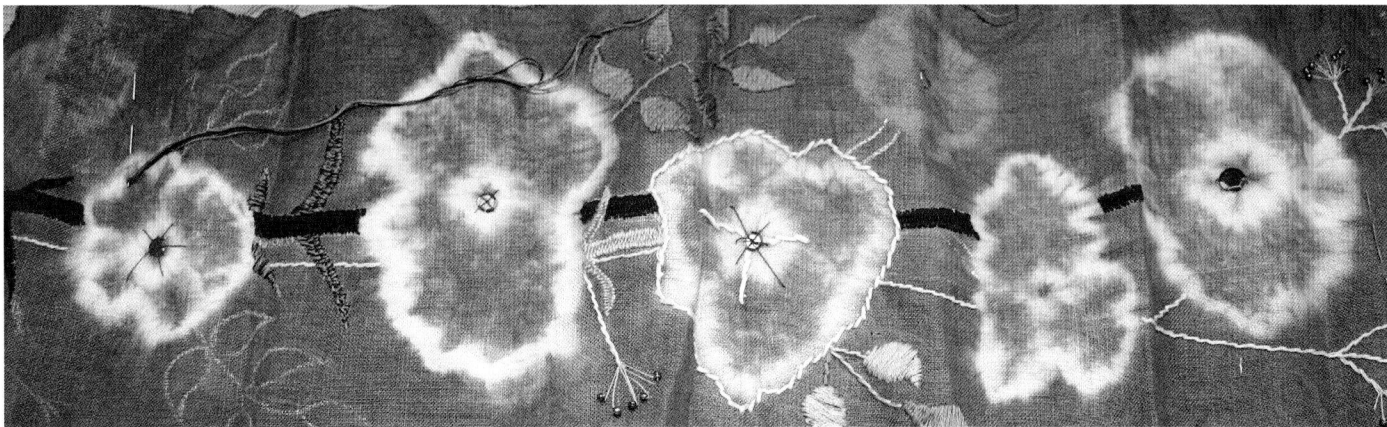

DIFFERENTIATION

Children who have not progressed as far...
These children can use rubber bands instead of string to create the marks on the fabric. Every child will get a result with the tie and dye process, but more individual responses should be encouraged, rather than just copying the example.

Children who have progressed further...
Ask these pupils to record how this process works, experimenting with techniques from different cultures, including using rice. They could try to create a more uniform design with the bunching and tying of the fabric or investigate other techniques for creating patterns using dye on fabric.

SESSION 3 **INVESTIGATING STITCHING**

LEARNING OBJECTIVES
Children will:

- develop skills and creativity by experimenting freely with a range of different stitches
- develop their technical skills and understanding by investigating stitches that relate to shape, colour, texture and pattern, with some form of accuracy
- start to understand the principles and techniques used in stitched textiles, using appropriate vocabulary
- develop their cultural understanding by learning about, comparing and commenting on the work of artists from different cultures.

VOCABULARY over and under, threading, stitching, embroidery, cross stitch, running stitch

RESOURCES

- a wide range of coloured embroidery thread or wool (from educational suppliers or fabric shops)
- felt squares, binca or fabric swatches (one per child)
- needles (one per child) – the size will depend on children's previous experience and the fabric (if using felt or binca, use large blunt needles; if using cotton, use a sharper needle)
- CD ROM: images of embroidery from around the world
- resource sheets: Stitching; Indian textile designs

ACTIVITY

Embroidery is a means of decorating fabric, one of its more simple methods being the *running stitch* – the thread passes in and out of the fabric giving a broken line. It can also be used to 'tack' or join fabric together temporarily. It is an important introduction to sewing and can be adapted easily for a range of purposes.

- Show the children the images on the CD-ROM of embroidery from around the world. Wall hangings, quilts, marriage gowns and cloth are embroidered, appliquéd, decorated with beadwork and embellished with mirrors, sequins, buttons and shells. Look at Chinese embroidery, English

- Ask pupils to bring in examples of embroidery or stitching that they have at home. If possible, supplement with samplers and embroidery from clothes, upholstery, shoes and handbags to share with the class.
- Discuss the types of stitch they can see. Ask, *Can you find running stitch, chain stitch, cross stitch, herringbone stitch?* If possible, find someone to talk to the children about embroidery (someone in the school or community may be an expert and could share their knowledge). Discuss how these items were made – by machine or hand – how old they are and how you can tell, and any history or stories they reveal.

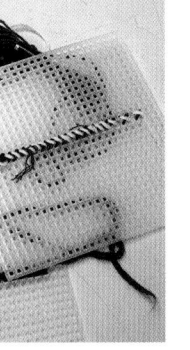

cross stitch, Japanese *Sashiko* embroidery and *Burkhani* (wedding scarves) from Gujarat in India. During the 17th century, Gujarat was one of the most important commercial embroidery centres in the world. Today, this area remains a very rich source of folk embroidery.

- Using binca, felt squares or scraps of fabric, start with the running stitch and ask pupils to practise creating their initial. (In advance of this, you will need to share how to thread a needle, start off in the fabric with a knot and finish off at the end or change colour.)

> **! HEALTH & SAFETY**
>
> Pupils will need to be shown how to handle needles carefully and made aware of the inherent dangers.

■ Only when this is mastered, move on to introducing other stitches. Enlarge and laminate the **Stitching** resource sheet and give the diagram to groups of children. Encourage them to experiment with the stitch shown in the diagram and then swap with other groups.

■ Bring the groups together to discuss any problems that might have arisen and to look at the samples of stitches that each group has created. Add these to sketchbooks with annotations of what they are called and how easy or difficult the children found this task. Ask them to grade each stitch with a score for difficulty from 1 to 5 and to explain why.

■ Using the designs collected in the gallery (Session 1) or the images from the **Indian textile designs** resource sheet, ask pupils to design a simple motif that they could then create in one of the stitches they have explored.

■ Pupils should draw their design onto fabric, felt or binca with a pencil or pen, making sure it is not too small or it will be difficult to control. Encourage each child to select an appropriate colour to use to create the stitches and to have a go at following their pattern using a running stitch, or other stitches if they are more confident.

■ Finally, bring the class together in a plenary to look at the finished pieces and discuss the designs, talking about which ones worked well, who found the stitching difficult, and why. Ask pupils, *Is it harder to stitch straight lines or curves?*

▼ **ASSESSMENT FOR LEARNING**

Can the children:

▸ discover, invent and use different stitches and master sewing a running stitch?

▸ create a range of different stitches and use them to create a pattern?

▸ recognise running, chain, blanket and cross stitch, and use appropriate vocabulary to describe their work?

▸ identify and talk about the qualities of different types of stitching and textile design from around the world?

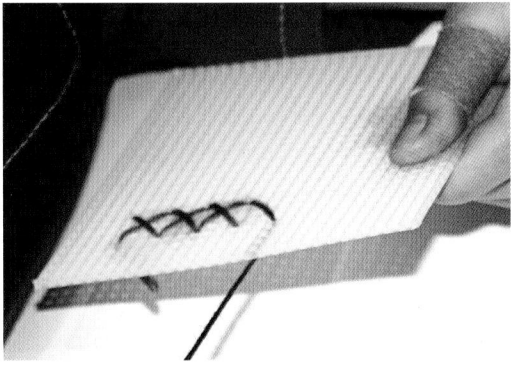

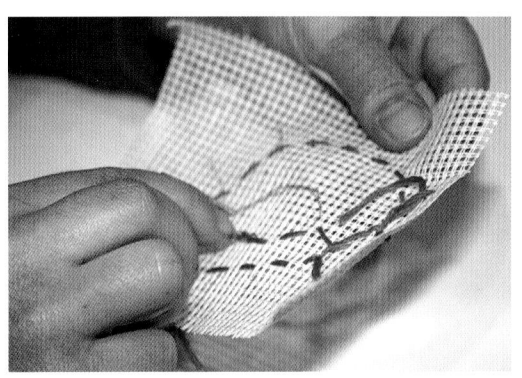

DIFFERENTIATION

Children who have not progressed as far…
These pupils can use a larger needle, depending on fine motor skill ability, and binca if they are struggling with the stitches. Ensure they have mastered the running stitch before you move on to any other stitch. Use a timer to encourage concentration.

Children who have progressed further…
More dexterous children could be encouraged to use a range of stitches or different coloured threads and combine them to create their own more complex design. Encourage research into other stitches used in embroidery. They could use a running stitch to decorate a T-shirt.

SESSION 4 **BUTTERFLY COLLAGES**

LEARNING OBJECTIVES

Children will:

- learn to experiment purposefully when designing their own imaginative butterfly collage
- work from images in the natural world and develop skills in overlapping, ripping, pattern and colour

- use a sketchbook and series of experiments to plan a collage and evaluate their work
- further their understanding of other artists and craftspeople by studying how they have used collage.

VOCABULARY antennae, proboscis, caterpillar, cocoon, metamorphosis, pupa, chrysalis, extinct, entomologist, rip, layer, overlap, contrast, symmetrical, pattern

▼ RESOURCES

- ▶ sketchbooks
  (one per child)
- ▶ black pens, pencils,
  crayons, oil pastels
- ▶ A4 and A3 cartridge paper
  (one sheet per child)
- ▶ Brusho, inks or
  watercolours for
  each table
- ▶ brushes – fine nylon hair,
  assorted sizes from 0–8
- ▶ mixing palettes –
  must be very clean
- ▶ water pots
  (one per table or child)
- ▶ empty boxes
  (lids of photocopier
  paper are ideal)
- ▶ selection of glossy
  magazines
- ▶ glue sticks
- ▶ CD-ROM:
  images of butterflies
- ▶ resource sheet:
  Butterflies
- ▶ pupil self-evaluation sheet

ACTIVITY

In this session, pupils will study butterflies as inspiration for a collage, which can then be used as the basis of a design in felt in Session 6. Prior to the session, collect together images of butterflies (from the **Butterflies** resource sheet, CD-ROM images, books and so on). Encourage pupils to bring in images of butterflies from home – they are often used on greetings cards or wrapping paper. If you can show pupils examples of real butterflies, this will really enhance the work. The **Pupil self-evaluation** sheet can be used to assess the work on this project.

■ Look at the selection of butterfly images with pupils and encourage them to use sketchbooks to record patterns, colours and shapes from the images (see Other Areas of Learning, page 58, for cross-curricular links).

Talk about symmetry in the wings. Invite them to use a range of drawing materials, such as pencil, black pen, crayon and oil pastels.

■ Encourage pupils to select details of the butterflies – wings, patterns, colours, body – and to draw these using oil pastels on A4 or A3 cartridge paper. Demonstrate how if you overlay a coloured wash in Brusho, ink or watercolour, the water repels the oil and the oil pastel shines through. Children could also create whole butterfly images if you have time.

■ Talk about collages with the class. What types of material could they use to create collages? What kinds of collage could they make?

■ Lay out a selection of empty boxes to collect colour samples (one per colour). Ask pupils to search through the glossy magazines looking for sections of colour that would represent

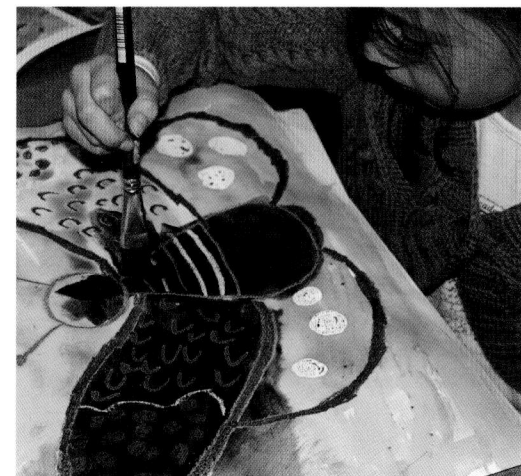

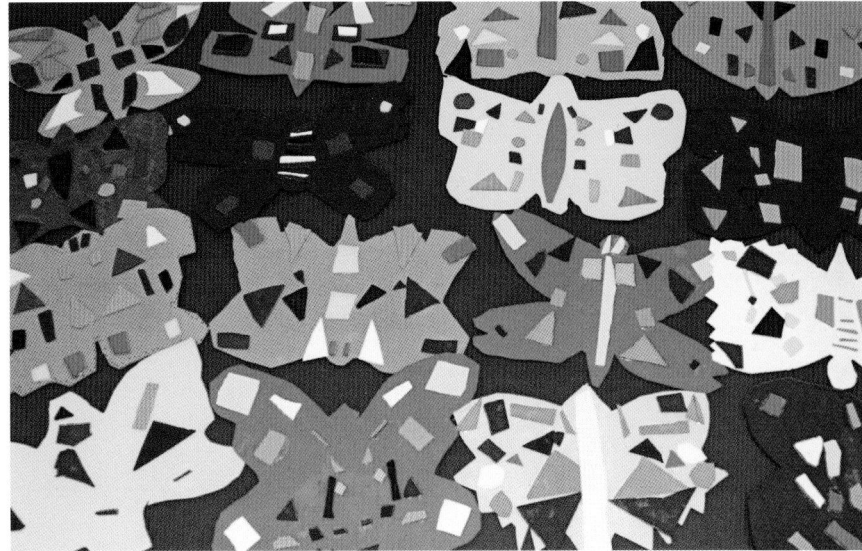

butterflies (some will be parts of pages; others full pages) and then add them to the appropriate box. After about ten minutes, you will have a huge array of colours to work from.

■ Using these colour samples, demonstrate how to rip the paper to give a rough edge, as well as how to overlap small pieces of paper. Ask pupils to create samples in their sketchbooks of different sections of a range of butterflies using the paper and a glue stick.

■ When the children feel confident, ask them to plan a design – either a whole butterfly or a pattern based on a part – on A4 or A3 paper and create a collage using the glossy paper overlapped, torn, cut and layered.

■ Find time in the session to discuss aspects that arise, review work at different stages and give the children a chance to talk about things they have discovered.

■ Show pupils examples of contemporary textile artist Patricia Greaves (see the CD-ROM), who uses a wide range of materials in her impressions of the sea. Discuss the way in which she uses lots of stitching and materials to create textile collages. Ask, *How could you create a textile collage of a butterfly? What type of materials could you use for wings, body, details and patterns?*

■ As an extension, pupils could be encouraged to design their own piece of work in the form of a collage butterfly, combining all the skills of this unit. They could use the tie-and-dye fabric from Session 2 and the stitching from Session 3, as well as adding embellishments in the form of sequins and beads.

▼ ASSESSMENT FOR LEARNING

Can the children:
▶ sketch sections of butterflies in a sketchbook, showing an understanding of symmetry?
▶ make marks with papers that suggest the features of a butterfly?
▶ use their initial drawings and experiments within their final piece of work and discuss the outcomes with a partner?
▶ talk about the work of an artist and how they have used collage?

DIFFERENTIATION

Children who have not progressed as far…
These pupils may find it helpful to use magnifying glasses to look for patterns. The activity could be broken into small achievable steps, such as finding and drawing two different wing patterns. Encourage them to practise ripping, layering and gluing in advance of the final piece.

Children who have progressed further…
Encourage free use of materials with these children. Observational drawings should focus their attention to detail. Use the extension ideas and encourage them to select from a range of different materials and incorporate stitches in their final work, referring back to Session 3.

SESSION 5 **MAKING FELT**

LEARNING OBJECTIVES
Children will:

- learn to explore, investigate and experiment by taking a raw material and making it into a piece of fabric
- learn to generate new ideas by working from nature to design and make a layer piece of felt, focusing on colour and pattern
- learn to work collectively and individually, commenting on their work and helping others
- learn about the importance of hand-made fabrics.

VOCABULARY shrunken, wool tops, carded wool, tease, matting, friction, line, colour, pattern, pressure, criss-cross, overlap, wring out, stretch

▼ RESOURCES

- ▸ shrunken woollen jumper
- ▸ examples of felt – bags, hats, shoes (if available), machine-made felt squares or Fuzzy Felt
- ▸ bamboo mat (one per child) – use cut-up beach mats, bamboo table mats or sushi mats
- ▸ piece of netting (one per child) – cut-up old net curtain, slightly bigger than the bamboo mat
- ▸ piece of fabric (one per child) just larger than the bamboo mat – cut-up calico or old tea towels
- ▸ jugs of warm or hot water and containers for pouring
- ▸ washing-up liquid
- ▸ carded wool tops – un-dyed for first layers and a range of colours for detail (merino wool is best)
- ▸ old towels (for mopping), buckets (for wringing out or rinsing)
- ▸ Presentation: Making felt Masterclass
- ▸ CD-ROM: images of felt from around the world; images of felt textile works by contemporary artists, including Patricia Greaves
- ▸ pupil self-evaluation sheet

ACTIVITY

Felt was probably one of the first woollen fabrics. It is used in Europe, Asia, Africa and South America in a range of thicknesses to make warm boots, hats, coats, rugs and coverings for tents. In this session, pupils will create a piece of felt that could be used in a range of ways. You can use the butterfly designs from Session 4 as a starting point, but don't worry if they change when created. Prior to the session, look at and discuss the work of a contemporary textile artist, such as Patricia Greaves.

■ Discuss with the class how fibres can be criss-crossed or overlapped to create strength. This is a good time to make links to any weaving the children have done before (see *Art Express* Books 1 and 2).

■ Talk about what happens when a woollen jumper goes in a washing machine on a hot wash. This is the felting process – hot water, soap and friction will make a hand-made fabric out of wool fibres.

■ Before making felt, explore the subject matter for your felt design. This session has used butterflies as inspiration. Focusing on patterns, colours and shapes should give you successful results. Encourage pupils

to spend time sketching from images of butterflies in sketchbooks. (See Other Areas of Learning, page 58, for cross-curricular links.)

■ Familiarise yourself with the Masterclass, but do not show the children the whole process at this time. It is better to demonstrate each stage to the class yourself.

! HEALTH & SAFETY
Check for any allergies to wool or lanolin.

■ Start by demonstrating how to tease the wool out of the long length using your fingers, and how to build up alternate layers of wool that run lengthways and then across. The cheapest way of doing this is to use un-dyed wool for the first four layers and then colour for the detail, as coloured wool is more expensive.

■ At the end of the layering stage, cover the wool and mat with a piece of netting. If a child's wool has spread over the mat, help them tuck it in so all the wool is contained on the mat and under the net. If you are running out of time, stop at this stage and save work in a pile for the next lesson.

■ Move on to the hot water and soap stage (washing-up liquid is fine and easy to dispense). Add a small amount of soap and warm water and rub from the centre out. Sing songs as you rub. Encourage pupils to make sure their work goes flat and that all the wool is joined together by rubbing over any areas with lots of coloured details (lines, balls and so on).

■ Follow the Masterclass for the final stages. Spend time going over the process and looking at all the results.

Compare the size of the final pieces with the mat to find out how much the wool has shrunk. Use images from the CD-ROM to look at and discuss the work of contemporary artists.

■ When you have washed and dried the felt, combine the skills from previous sessions and add sequins, buttons and beads, or stitching to embellish. The final pieces can be displayed as a large group hanging if sewn together, made into book covers or purses, or placed in a frame as a gift.

■ At the end of the session, ask pupils to complete the **Pupil self-evaluation** sheet to provide feedback on the project.

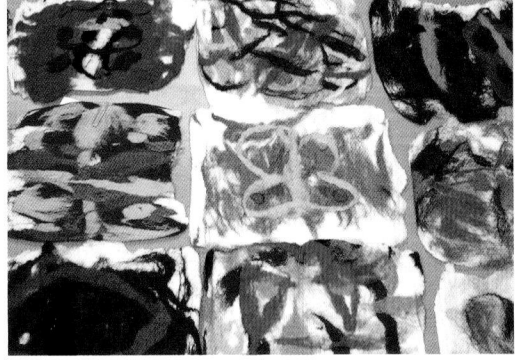

▼ ASSESSMENT FOR LEARNING

Can the children:
▶ play with wool tops to create a new piece of fabric?
▶ use butterflies for inspiration with colour and pattern and show evidence of these in their final work?
▶ help their peers throughout the activity, making suggestions if others are stuck or unsure of the process?

DIFFERENTIATION

Children who have not progressed as far...
The magic of felting is that all children will get an end result, even if they do not create an even surface. Make sure these children see your demonstration and keep the focus short (for example, *Ask me to take a look when you have done another layer*).

Children who have progressed further...
Encourage these pupils to create marks and images that really reflect butterflies, adapting the lines and marks with the wool and techniques shown. Encourage them not to jump ahead, but to spend time adding in details and using a wide range of tones and layers.

! HEALTH & SAFETY
Make sure the water is not boiling. (Children's hands are more sensitive than adults'.)

OTHER AREAS OF LEARNING

CROSS-CURRICULAR IDEAS

- SCIENCE AND GEOGRAPHY – The life cycle of a butterfly, endangered butterflies and conservation.
- LITERACY – Imagining life as a butterfly, life cycles and lots of wonderful butterfly and caterpillar stories, especially *The Very Hungry Caterpillar* by Eric Carle.
- DANCE AND DRAMA – Inspired by butterfly movements.
- MATHEMATICS – Symmetry, measuring, recording and investigating.

RECORDING AND INVESTIGATING

- Collect images of butterflies from magazines, books and the internet.
- Research different types of butterfly, particularly the differences between tropical and European species.
- Use sketchbooks to record butterfly shapes. Tear butterfly silhouettes out of folded black sugar paper.
- Record the wing patterns of different butterfly species.

Butterflies
(Collage & Textiles)

TOPICS TO EXPLORE WITH CHILDREN

- Investigate the life cycle of a butterfly.
- Which butterflies have camouflage and why might they need it?
- Why are some butterflies poisonous and others not?
- Find out about butterflies native to Britain.
- Organise a butterfly survey in the garden or school grounds. Collate information over a few weeks, especially on sunny days.
- Find out what plants butterflies are attracted to.

BACKGROUND

- Butterflies are one of the most beautiful, distinctive and easily recognised flying insects in the natural world. They come in a wealth of colours, patterns, shapes and sizes, making them an ideal starting point for a range of art projects in the classroom. The study of butterflies helps pupils gain an understanding of the world around them and of the beautiful and complex patterns that have evolved in nature.

BUTTERFLY FACTS

Encourage pupils to research butterfly facts, such as:

- Butterflies have four wings, which all flap together
- Their wings are covered in tiny scales
- They feed on juices from flowers or fruit through a thin, long tube called a proboscis
- The smallest butterfly in the world is called the Western Pygmy Blue from the USA, with a wing span of up to 2cm.

WEBSITES AND RESOURCES

- www.butterfly-conservation.org
- www.britishbutterflies.co.uk
- www.countrysideinfo.co.uk/butterfl.htm
- www.ukbutterflies.co.uk
- www.northamptonshirewildlife.co.uk
- www.nhm.ac.uk (Natural History Museum)
- *Caterpillars and Butterflies*
  Stephanie Turnbull (Usborne Beginners)
- *Butterflies and Moths of Britain and Europe*
  Helga Hofmann, Thomas Marktanner
  (Collins Nature Guides)
- *Britain's Butterflies*
  David Tomlinson, Rob Still (Wild Guides)

Many sculptures are made of clay. Clay has also been used as an important building material for many civilisations, from 7000 years ago in Mesopotamia (now Iraq), through Ancient Egypt and the Romans to the present day. By looking at how clay has been used by different cultures throughout time and in the local environment, pupils will develop an understanding of their own history and how people lived in the past. There are rich and diverse examples of the uses of clay in local buildings and children will be introduced to some of the different functions of clay, from bricks to drainage pipes.

Prior to Year 3, pupils will have explored the sensory qualities of clay. They will have begun to develop basic modelling and construction techniques, employing clay tools for different purposes, and have used observation to represent forms three-dimensionally. Pupils will have discovered the possibilities of clay by exploring it, developing their ideas and looking at sculptures from different cultures.

During this unit, children will investigate the local environment, collecting information about form, shape, texture, colour and pattern of buildings or landscape through sketchbook research. They will experiment with techniques and ideas, applying and refining their skills. They will concentrate on the various details, becoming more confident in using the visual and tactile elements, applying clay skills of joining, building and subtracting, and improving control of tools to inscribe surfaces.

Pupils will use a specialist vocabulary to evaluate their work. They will also enhance their critical awareness, by looking at and describing how materials such as clay have been used, and in addition, they will develop an understanding of its significant role throughout history.

AIMS
This unit offers children the opportunity to:
■ explore and create by collecting and selecting visual research from first-hand observation and other sources to develop ideas for their work
■ investigate and use the qualities of materials and processes to develop practical skills of modelling and construction, extending their control of tools and processes and evaluating their suitability for different tasks
■ develop critical skills by adapting and refining their own work in line with the limitations and possibilities of materials and processes
■ develop an understanding of architecture, both local and from other cultures, by comparison of different materials, approaches and technologies over time.

ASSESSMENT FOR LEARNING
During this unit, you should look for evidence of progress through observation, discussion and practical work. Pupils should be exploring and developing ideas for their work by purposefully selecting information from sketchbook research. Responses should show that they have developed confidence to use tools to create specific effects, and have investigated and applied modelling techniques to communicate their ideas. Assess children's ability to use their understanding and knowledge about local architecture to adapt and improve their work.

▶ **CD-ROM RESOURCES**

Artworks and images
Resource sheets:
    Investigating the local environment
    Exploring surface texture
    Looking at buildings
    Architecture from other times and places
    Brickwork in the local environment
    Examples of bas relief – The Elgin Marbles
Teacher assessment
Pupil self-evaluation

SESSION 1 INVESTIGATING THE LOCAL ENVIRONMENT

LEARNING OBJECTIVES
Children will:
- develop their skills of observation and extend vocabulary by describing and comparing the properties of different building materials
- develop their practical skills of recording by selecting and drawing from first-hand observation of the environment.

VOCABULARY viewpoint, viewfinder, detail, decoration, natural, symmetry, form, two-dimensional, three-dimensional, relief (raised surface), materials, surfaces, tiles, brick, slate, wood, stone, metal, bronze, iron, hard/soft, rough/smooth, shiny/dull, flat/bumpy, rounded, hollow, architect, bas relief

▼ RESOURCES

- ▸ building materials, such as bricks of different colours, a piece of slate, tiles, clay drainage pipe, clay chimney pot, wood with different grains, marble (some examples on the CD-ROM)
- ▸ sketchbooks
- ▸ soft, coloured pencils in a variety of colours
- ▸ viewfinders
- ▸ digital cameras
- ▸ 2B and 4B pencils
- ▸ thick black wax crayons for rubbing surface textures
- ▸ newsprint for rubbings
- ▸ resource sheet: Investigating the local environment

> **! HEALTH & SAFETY**
>
> Ensure adequate numbers of adults accompany the class, to supervise working on location.

ACTIVITY

In this session, a series of short activities will focus pupils on the properties of different materials they will encounter when investigating buildings. Introduce the unit by explaining to the class that they will be looking at and collecting information about landscape or buildings in the local environment to create a bas relief (a surface projecting only slightly from its background) in clay. The experience of making colour notes and experimenting with viewfinders will give pupils the tools to collect good-quality information in their sketchbooks.

■ As an initial stimulus, provide a range of building materials. Ask the children to discuss the properties of the materials. Ask, *Are they heavy or light? What are they made from? Are they formed from natural materials? Can you think how they were made? Where might they be found on a building?* Revise the word *texture*. Invite pupils to feel and describe the textures of the materials. Ask them to look at the different colours of the bricks. Do the colours differ? Why? As an introduction to making colour notes in their sketchbooks, ask them to use soft, coloured pencils to mix and match the colours of some of the objects supplied, or to annotate detail.

■ Introduce viewfinders and explain that their purpose is to select interesting features or an area to draw. Ask pupils to experiment with the viewfinders by walking around the classroom selecting areas to focus on. Encourage them to explore what happens when they move closer to something or further away, and when they hold the viewfinder vertically or horizontally. (Viewfinders can be made

from a card frame 3–5cm wide or from a plastic slide mount. Make sure pupils hold the viewfinder in front of their eye so that it successfully frames what they see.)

■ Arrange a walk around the local environment identifying interesting buildings or features of the landscape. Point out architectural features and sculptures on buildings. The **Investigating the local environment** resource sheet gives examples of

questions to extend the children's looking and learning. Collect photographic images of the buildings. These can be used as stimulus in a classroom display and as a basis for discussion in Session 4.

■ Explain to pupils that they are to use a viewfinder to either draw particular features of a landscape or building, or to select part of a building in their sketchbooks. Ask them to spend time looking carefully, then draw the main shapes and forms, adding details of pattern and texture. As the drawings develop, focus their attention on the patterns of bricks, tiles and so on.

■ Finally, ask pupils to collect information about colour by making colour notes in their sketchbooks. Ensure the class has sufficient time to collect the information. If this is not possible in one session, arrange a follow-up visit. For additional visual information, ask each child to take a photograph of either the area they are drawing or particular details.

■ It is important pupils work directly from buildings or the landscape in their sketchbooks to make a personal response to the real thing, rather than working from inferior secondary source materials, such as photographs. These tend to give a one-dimensional view. Photographs may be used as reference when making the clay relief.

Can the children:
▶ compare and describe the properties of different building materials using appropriate vocabulary?
▶ use a viewfinder to select a particular area?
▶ record the local environment from observation, drawing basic shapes, adding details of pattern and texture independently or extending visual research?

DIFFERENTIATION

Children who have not progressed as far...
When working on location, encourage pupils with shorter concentration spans to select one feature of a building or landscape, such as a doorway or a window. To extend their looking, you will need to ask focused questions, for example: *Are all the window panes the same size? How are the bricks joined together?*

Children who have progressed further...
To extend the activity and make it more challenging, ask these children to imagine what might happen to the building or landscape five minutes later – for example, the window may open, a person may look out or a cat might go to sleep on the windowsill. Ask pupils to jot down or draw ideas in their sketchbooks. Children could extend research at home by drawing extra objects from observation, such as curtains blowing in the wind.

SESSION 2 EXPLORING SURFACE TEXTURE

LEARNING OBJECTIVES
Children will:
- develop their control of tools and basic techniques using clay
- learn to investigate and explore ideas for surface textures and patterns created using natural and man-made objects.

VOCABULARY texture, pattern, line, bang, flatten, smooth, scratch, roll, coil; words to describe clay: **leather-hard, plastic**

▼ RESOURCES

- ▶ school buff clay
- ▶ rolling pins
- ▶ guides (short lengths of wood, 1cm thick)
- ▶ A3 sugar paper (easy to clear up)
- ▶ protective clothing
- ▶ collection of made and natural objects, such as buttons, key, screws, cogs, Lego bricks, hair combs, cord, sea shells, fir cones, twigs
- ▶ textured surfaces, such as woven baskets, grids, patterns on the soles of shoes, tyres, bark
- ▶ clay tools (plastic and wooden)
- ▶ kitchen sieve or garlic press
- ▶ resource sheet: Exploring surface texture

> **! HEALTH & SAFETY**
>
> Care should be taken to avoid making clay dust. Inhaling fine particles is extremely dangerous to health. Surfaces and the floor should be wiped with a damp cloth – avoid brushing, which causes dust.

ACTIVITY

Introduce the purpose of the session, which is to explore pattern and experiment with surface texture by subtracting from the surface of the clay and building upon it. For this activity the clay will need to be 'leather-hard' so that it maintains its shape. If the clay is 'plastic' (soft), leave it out in the air until the moisture evaporates. It should then become slightly firmer and keep its shape.

■ Demonstrate to the class how to roll out a flat piece of clay. Two strips of wood, 1 cm thick, placed one each side of the clay will help pupils to roll out clay to an even thickness. Clay should be flattened with the heel of the hand – encourage the children to press down

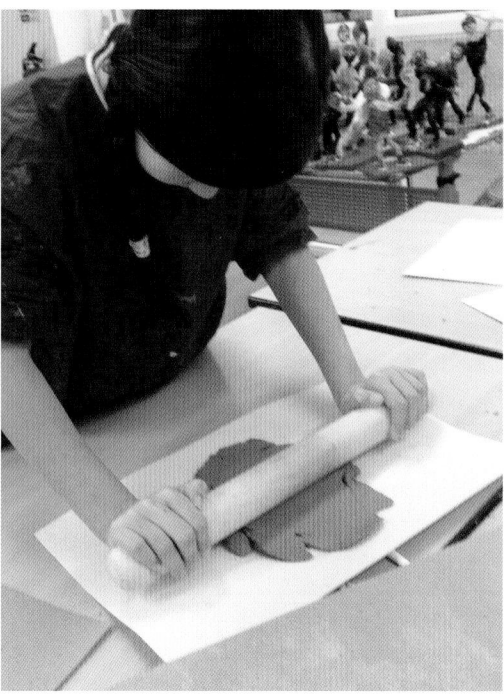

on the clay, not to bang it. Then show them how to press the rolling pin down and roll out, away from the body, repeating until the clay is the same thickness as the guides. Make sure the children stand up to roll out the clay so they can apply even pressure. (Pupils can work on a piece of A3 sugar paper or wooden boards, rather than on a plastic table, which the clay will stick to.)

■ When the children have rolled their slabs of clay, give them collections of made and natural objects to press into the surface to explore the patterns they can make. Ask the children to experiment, making impressions using different parts of one object. Encourage pupils to touch the impressions and to talk to each other about the variety in the patterns they have made. They might like to guess the objects that made each other's patterns. Can they describe how they made their own patterns? Record experiments on the **Exploring surface texture** resource sheet. This activity will provide a reference that may be used as a source of ideas when making the clay relief.

■ Make available a range of textured surfaces. Remind pupils how they made clay cuboids (see *Art Express* Book 2). Then ask them to make impressions by pressing the clay onto the textured surface. Allow the cubes to dry overnight. These can be used as a resource to stamp textures. To extend this activity, some children may like to experiment further by pushing soft clay through a kitchen sieve or garlic press.

■ Ask the children to roll out a flat piece of clay. Provide a variety of clay tools for them to experiment with making textures and patterns. Encourage pupils to press the tool into the depth of the clay rather than scratching the surface. When experimenting, ask them to use the side or point of the clay tool to make different marks. Record experiments on the **Exploring surface texture** resource sheet. These experiences will provide references to use as a source of ideas when making the clay relief.

■ Finally, explore with pupils different ways of making coils. For this activity the clay needs to be soft and pliable. Children will need practice to make coils of an even thickness. This is easier if they roll the clay with both hands on a flat surface. Suggest that they may wish to develop ideas for using coils from the sketchbook research, for railings, gates and so on.

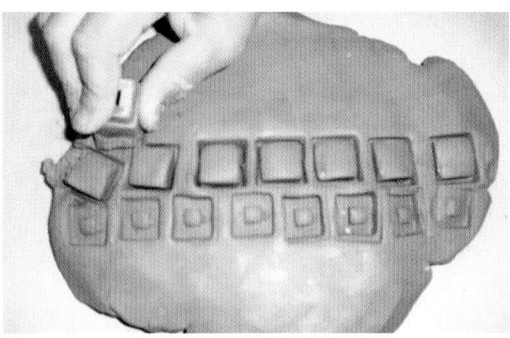

■ Clay used in these activities can be recycled, although you may like to retain a couple of examples to use as exemplar material in Session 3. Remind pupils how to push all the pieces of clay together to make a large cube, and make a large hole in the middle with their thumb. This can be filled with water and will ensure the clay stays plastic. The clay cubes should be stored in an airtight plastic container or a plastic bag.

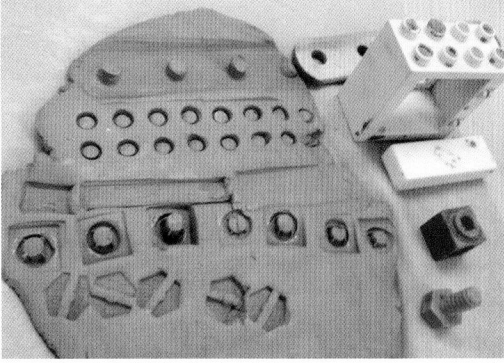

▼ ASSESSMENT FOR LEARNING

Can the children:
▶ roll out a flat piece of clay of an even thickness, independently or with support?
▶ investigate and explore a range of ideas for surface textures using natural and made objects?

DIFFERENTIATION

Children who have not progressed as far...
Exploring the surface texture of made and natural objects is an ideal time to introduce new vocabulary and verbs to pupils with English as an additional language or poor language skills. Language can be used to accompany actions. This will support both the understanding and use of English.

Children who have progressed further...
Extend these children's experience by asking them to experiment further, contrasting the marks made with tools of different shapes and thickness. Ask them to describe the different textures they make.

SESSION 3 BUILDING UP THE CLAY BAS RELIEF

LEARNING OBJECTIVES
Children will:

- learn to express and develop ideas for a clay relief of the environment using sketchbook research
- develop practical skills by exploring construction techniques for joining clay
- learn to review their work as it progresses and describe how to develop their work further.

VOCABULARY **shape, form, colour, pattern, texture, hard, soft, rough, smooth, bumpy, prickly, ridged, slip, thumb pot, modelling, constructing**

▼ RESOURCES

- ▶ sketchbook research from Session 1
- ▶ school buff clay
- ▶ cutting wire
- ▶ rolling pins
- ▶ guides (short lengths of wood, 1cm thick)
- ▶ A3 sugar paper (one per child)
- ▶ protective clothing
- ▶ sharp pencils
- ▶ clay tools (plastic and wooden)
- ▶ blunt knives (not with serrated edges)
- ▶ fine plant spray
- ▶ resource sheet: Examples of bas relief – The Elgin Marbles

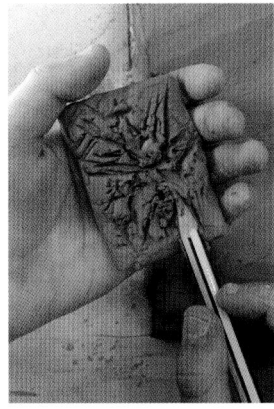

▶ INFORMATION
You may wish to teach the next session within a week to prevent the clay drying out, although if it is carefully wrapped and airtight, this should not happen.

ACTIVITY

You may wish to block time for this session, as pupils may need an extended period of time to develop their work. Before the session, check the consistency of the clay is 'leather-hard', in other words that it is firm and keeps its shape. If the clay work is to be fired later, use the clay directly from the bag to ensure there are no air bubbles, which could cause trouble firing. Slabs of clay can be cut easily (by adults only) with a cutting wire.

■ Explain to the children that they are going to recreate a bas relief of a building or part of the landscape using their sketchbook research from Session 1. They can begin by rolling out a flat piece of clay using the wooden guides. Pupils may need to turn the clay around if it becomes too long and thin. Deter them from rolling backwards and forwards as this just tends to move the clay, rather than making it thinner.

■ Referring to their original sketchbook drawing, ask pupils to use a pencil to lightly draw the outline of the building on the surface of their clay slab. Then ask them to cut out the main shape of the building or the landscape. At this point they can lightly draw the shapes of the roof, windows or other features onto the building or landscape.

■ Revise and demonstrate to the class how to join clay using the scratch and slip method. (Show the Masterclass from *Art Express* Book 1 or 2 to the children, if necessary) Make a thumb pot and tap the bottom to make it flat. Fill the pot with water. To join two pieces of clay, scratch or crosshatch both surfaces with a tool or pencil. Dip your finger into the water and rub around the rim of the thumb pot to make a slip. Cover both surfaces with slip and press together. If the textures flatten, scratch again to roughen the surfaces. Remind pupils that clay simply pushed together will fall apart when dry.

▼ ASSESSMENT FOR LEARNING

Can the children:
▶ make a clay relief using ideas from sketchbook research independently, imaginatively or with support?
▶ apply techniques of joining pieces of clay to accomplish the task?
▶ indicate which parts of their work they like and dislike, and suggest ways of making improvements, giving reasons why?

■ Working from their drawings, ask the children to select the next largest shape. They will need to roll out a flat piece of clay thinner than their original slab. The shape can be drawn, cut out and joined onto the building using the scratch and slip method. Edges can be smoothed using fingers.

Deter pupils from adding water to smooth the clay as it will become slimy and difficult to manage. If the clay begins to dry out, spray the air around it using a plant spray – the clay will absorb the moisture from the air.

Explain to the class that smaller shapes of doors, window frames or other details of landscape can be added in the same way. Remind them of how they experimented with making rolls of clay. Can they think of any parts of the building they could make from coils, such as curved tiles, drainpipes or guttering?

■ In a plenary, ask pupils to talk to a partner about making their sculptures. Which part do they think is most successful? Which parts could be improved? Remind the children to look at the information in their sketchbooks.
■ To keep the work in good condition for the next session, place pupils' work individually in a damp cloth and store inside an airtight plastic bag. To keep the work flat, place on pieces of card for storage.

DIFFERENTIATION

Children who have not progressed as far...
Pupils who have coordination problems may need individual adult support to reinforce how to join the clay. Emphasise the importance of scratching the two surfaces well in order to make a good join. As the children work, it would be beneficial to discuss which parts of the building or landscape to build up first.

Children who have progressed further...
These children could work out ways to make their relief more three-dimensional – for example, making a bay window or chimney from smaller slabs of clay. During the plenary, they could feed back to the class how they solved the problem. They may also require extra time to add ideas developed in their sketchbooks.

SESSION 4 ADDING DETAILS OF PATTERN AND TEXTURE

LEARNING OBJECTIVES
Children will:

- develop the ability to use sketchbook research to lead their investigations and purposeful experiments
- learn to improve their control of tools and processes, refining their work by building on initial explorations of surface texture

- learn to evaluate their own and others' work
- develop knowledge and understanding of architecture, both local and from other cultures, by comparing how varied materials, approaches and technologies have been used over time.

VOCABULARY shape, form, colour, hard, soft, rough, smooth, rigid, pliable, cylinder, three-dimensional, cone, sphere, cube, cuboid, solid, hollow, malleable, leather-hard, dry, biscuit-fired, glazed, sculptor, sculpture, carving, modelling, constructing, kiln, slip

▾ RESOURCES

- ▸ display of photographs of buildings of different ages from the locality
- ▸ school buff clay
- ▸ A3 sugar paper (one per child)
- ▸ protective clothing
- ▸ clay tools (plastic and wooden)
- ▸ range of brushes, such as old paintbrushes, toothbrushes
- ▸ collection of made and natural objects
- ▸ kitchen sieve or garlic press
- ▸ resource sheets: Looking at buildings; Architecture from other times and places; Brickwork in the local environment

ACTIVITY

Look with pupils at the classroom display of images of interesting local buildings and features of the landscape. These might include buildings with decorative features such as Greek columns, Victorian civic buildings, the school building and places of worship. Images may also be projected onto a whiteboard and used as stimulus for discussion. Buildings from other cultures and times can be added to the display to extend the children's experiences (see the **Looking at buildings** and **Architecture from other times and places** resource sheets). Some children may make connections with how Greek and Roman architecture have influenced buildings in their environment.

■ During a class discussion, ask pupils to compare examples of local architecture. Ask, *Are the buildings old or new? Can you identify materials used in the buildings? How have they been used? What do you notice about the older*

buildings? Ask pupils to discuss with a partner what they think and feel about a particular building. Share ideas with the class. Compile a word-bank of materials to add to the wall display and put in sketchbooks, and include descriptions of the materials. Focus the children on the use of bricks and tiles in the building, particularly if they have been used in a decorative way – for example, around doors or on pathways (see the **Brickwork in the local environment** resource sheet).

■ Explain to pupils that they are to try out alternative ideas for textures and patterns on clay slabs, referring to their drawings and information in their sketchbooks (for example, tiles, bricks, foliage or fencing). Ask them to use clay tools to experiment with making textures and patterns on a flat slab of clay. Encourage them to try out a range of tools, pressing into the depth of the clay rather than scratching the surface. Provide a range

▸ INFORMATION
Dry sculptures slowly away from direct heat.

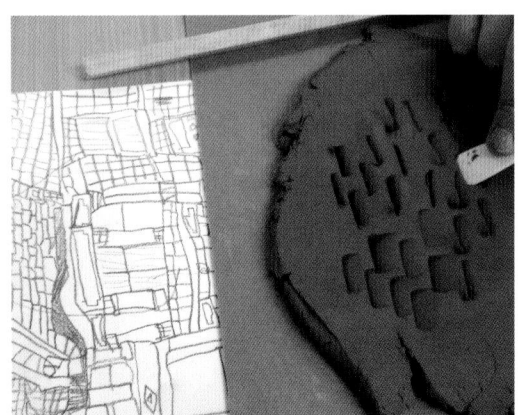

of brushes for them to experiment with making surface textures for cement, pebbledash and so on. Remind them of their experiments in Session 2.

■ Unwrap the children's work from Session 3 and, if it is too soft, leave the

pieces in the air to dry until they become firmer. Ask the children to add the textures and patterns to their clay relief, encouraging them to use a wide range of techniques and referring to their investigations. Make it clear that if they are not satisfied with the textures they create, they can change their work at any time as it progresses.

■ As a plenary, ask pupils to evaluate their work by talking about their investigations with a partner, focusing on the following questions: *What tools did you use to make the textures? What did you think about when selecting the tool or object? How appropriate were the textures or patterns you made? If you made a choice, can you explain why?*

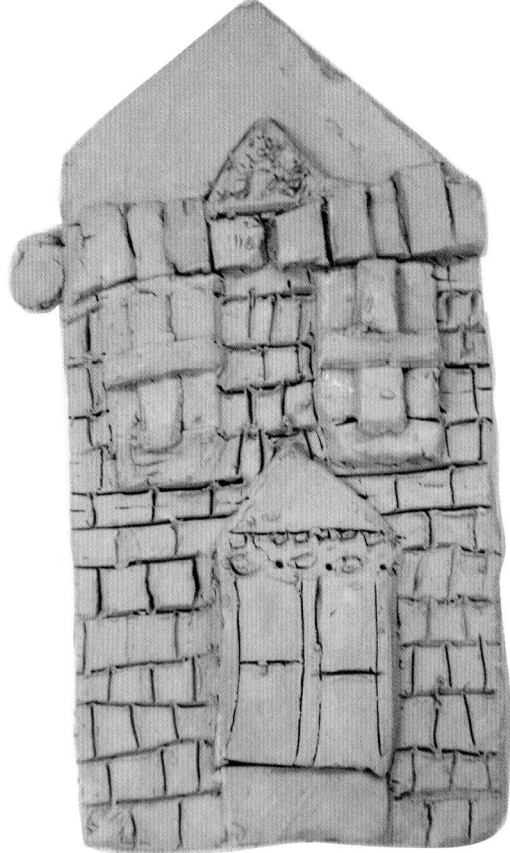

▼ ASSESSMENT FOR LEARNING

Can the children:

▶ make simple comments about observations, compare or talk about the differences in buildings, and show understanding of why these materials are used?

▶ use research to select appropriate tools or objects to represent a variety of textures and patterns for different parts of their relief?

▶ evaluate their own and others' work, describing and/or explaining why they chose certain tools or objects to inscribe surface texture?

▶ start to compare materials, approaches and technologies used locally and in other cultures and times?

DIFFERENTIATION

Children who have not progressed as far...
Organise adult support to focus these children's investigations, asking them to describe the textures or patterns in the drawings they wish to represent. If children have limited language skills or have English as an additional language, model descriptive language and provide visual support.

Children who have progressed further...
To extend reasoning skills, during discussions ask these pupils if they can explain why the architect used certain materials for the building. Challenge them to create surface textures in new and inventive ways.

SESSION 5 **ADDING COLOUR FROM SKETCHBOOK RESEARCH**

LEARNING OBJECTIVES

Children will:

- develop their practical skills by considering and applying colour to their sculpture from sketchbook research
- develop knowledge and understanding of the firing process

- develop their critical understanding and capacity to improve independently, commenting on their own work using a specialist vocabulary.

VOCABULARY **three-dimensional, cylinder, cone, sphere, cube, cuboid, solid, hollow, malleable, leather-hard, dry, biscuit-fired, glazed, sculptor, sculpture, carving, modelling, casting, constructing, kiln, slip**

▼ RESOURCES

- ▶ colour notes from sketchbook research
- ▶ photographs of buildings
- ▶ paint in the double primary system: vermillion and crimson; brilliant yellow and lemon yellow; Prussian blue and cobalt blue; plus white and turquoise
- ▶ mixing palettes
- ▶ water pots
- ▶ medium hog-hair and fine brushes (size 4 or 6)
- ▶ A4 white sugar paper (for testing colours)
- ▶ varnish or PVA glue
- ▶ lead free glazes
- ▶ clay in different states, plastic (malleable), dry, biscuit-fired and glazed
- ▶ pupil self-evaluation sheet

ACTIVITY

Ensure the clay from Session 4 is completely dry. Prior to the session, ask the class why the colour of the clay has changed. Inform the class that their work is fragile and will need careful handling. This session may be taught in two or three separate parts according to the time available.

■ Explain that the aim of this session is to add colour to their clay work from Session 4. The colour notes made in their sketchbooks and photographs will be used for reference.

Provide pupils with the double primary range of colours (see Resources). Ensure each child has their own mixing palette, water pot, medium-sized and fine brushes and an A4 test sheet to try out their colours. Demonstrate

how to mix colours – if the class have limited experience, organise a session for them to mix and match colours to the colour notes in their sketchbooks. Ask pupils to paint their clay relief carefully, trying out colours on a test sheet before they apply them onto their work. Focus the children on selecting the right-sized brush for the task.

■ At this stage the colours will appear rather chalky as the clay is porous, however, when the relief is varnished, the colours will become brighter. When the reliefs are dry, varnish them with a clear water-based varnish or PVA glue. Two or three coats will help to strengthen the clay.

■ Give pupils clay in different states – plastic (malleable),

leather-hard, dry, biscuit-fired and glazed. Clay plant pots can be used as an example of fired clay. Cups and plates may be used as examples of clay that has been glazed.

■ Ask pupils what the differences are in the clay. Show them some clay that has been fired, and introduce the term *biscuit-fired*. Compare a glazed piece of clay. What is the difference? Discuss the process of firing clay and provide pictorial support (books, posters) to show the firing process. Introduce new vocabulary, such as *kiln* and *firing*.

■ If you have access to a kiln in your school, show pupils the loaded kiln. Explain how high the temperature of the kiln will become and the length of time the pieces will need to become fired. Biscuit-fire the work. When cool, provide lead-free glazes for the children to glaze their work. Dispense small quantities into a mixing palette.

Start with white and lighter colours – colours may be mixed for more subtle shades. To make colours darker and richer, it is advisable to use other dark colours, such as brown or dark blue. Fire work a second time.

■ Ask pupils to evaluate their work, sharing ideas in a class discussion. Ask, *How did you select a building/landscape to work from? What did you find interesting? What do you think you have improved at during this activity? Can you explain how experimenting with clay helped develop your work? What challenges did you face? How did you overcome them? Which part of your work is most successful and why? How do you think you could make your work better?*

■ At the end of the session, provide each child with the **Pupil self-evaluation** sheet for feedback on the work undertaken in the unit.

▼ ASSESSMENT FOR LEARNING

Can the children:
▶ mix and match colours accurately from sketchbook research?
▶ describe the firing process and show some understanding that the changes are irreversible?
▶ explain the skills they have developed, identifying successful aspects of their work and areas to develop in future work?

DIFFERENTIATION

Children who have not progressed as far...
Encourage these pupils to wait for colours to dry before painting adjacent colours. When evaluating their work, adult support could help them extend their thinking. Provide word-banks and visual support for children with English as an additional language.

Children who have progressed further...
These children can work together to produce a booklet about firing clay, explaining how the changes are irreversible. Digital photographs could be inserted. This could be used as a resource for the class. Give the children extra time to refine their work by painting details. When evaluating their work, encourage them to make connections with architecture they have studied.

OTHER AREAS OF LEARNING

SCIENCE

■ Links can be made with the topics of 'Rocks and soils' and 'Characteristics of materials'. Pupils can learn about the properties of clay by looking at how it has been used in different ways.

GEOGRAPHY

■ Pupils can use buildings as a focus for a local study. They can record the changes that have taken place over time both by looking at the age of buildings and through examining local maps. They could observe and record where buildings are located and identify their use.

■ From this local study, children could explore conservation issues, such as preserving the local aging buildings. They could look at improvements in the environment and the impact they make.

HISTORY

■ Links may be made with the history topic 'How did the Romans change Britain when they settled here?' By arranging a visit to a Roman site or Roman remains in the locality, pupils can investigate evidence of Roman occupation. They could research how clay was used in everyday life through examining buildings, villas, pottery and roads, leading to an understanding of the Roman lifestyle.

■ Pupils can investigate how clay bricks were used to build Tudor houses, and they can examine internal and external features, such as fireplaces and chimneys. They could compare differences between houses built in Tudor times and today, as well as considering which types of building have survived and why.

■ Children could look at street names, which may reveal the existence of brick- and tile-making sites in the past – for example, Brick Lane or Clayponds Avenue. Pupils could extend their research by using the archives at the local library.

Sculpture

RELIGIOUS EDUCATION

■ Identify and record features from places of worship in the local environment to develop an understanding of how they reflect different religions and how faith is an inspiration to create something beautiful.

■ Pupils could explore the stylised shapes and patterns of natural forms depicted on Islamic tiles. They could make their own designs developed from drawings of natural forms. They could then make their own tiles from clay.

ICT

■ From geographical and historical research of the local area, children could combine text and graphics to produce either a class booklet about the local area or a multimedia presentation. Digital photographs and drawings made on location could be scanned and combined with relevant text. Pupils could work in groups to research different aspects of the environment. Conservation issues could be added.

■ Studies from observation of brick patterns and other features of buildings could be used as a basis for developing images using a repeating pattern.

By the age of seven, pupils will make drawings and paintings from memory, imagination and observation. They will explore tools and media, and begin to experiment with scale and detail. However, computer software that is controlled by a mouse is not the most sensitive of drawing and painting implements. In design studios, graphics tablets (a small drawing board with an electronic pen that enables artists to work in a more natural way) are often used. These are not generally available in primary schools. Therefore, working with and modifying digital photographs using a mouse adds a new dimension to children's art experience and is more appropriate than trying to draw realistic images on a computer screen. Using ICT in art and design does not, therefore, replace work done with traditional media but adds another set of tools that can be used in different ways to challenge children's creativity.

Prior to Year 3, pupils will have had the opportunity to use computer tools in different ways and should be familiar with the basics of opening, closing and saving images, drawing and painting on screen, as well as modifying and adding detail to digital photographs and drawings.

In this unit, pupils will have the opportunity to explore and extend their use of digital tools, particularly the use of layers to manipulate photographs in different and creative ways. They will learn how creative professionals use layers, and how to develop imaginative digital collages and fantasy pictures based on photographs. The sessions have been organised as a sequence so that the experiences build over a period of time. Session 1 stands alone and is an introduction to layers, while Sessions 2 and 3 go together. Sessions 4 and 5 go together but Session 4 could be used as a stand-alone session. The sessions

should last 30–50 minutes but you should be flexible, depending on the experience of the children.

To complete the work in this unit, you will need image-manipulation software that has layers, such as *Photoshop Elements*, which is a relatively inexpensive yet powerful software package. You can download a trial version from the Adobe website at www.adobe.com/uk.

AIMS

This unit offers children the opportunity to:
- extend their knowledge of digital tools and processes to experiment with image-making
- learn how to use layers to create both collage and fantasy images
- begin to develop an understanding of the ways in which digital image-making is used by professionals to create exciting images.

ASSESSMENT FOR LEARNING

During the unit, you should look for growing confidence in the ways that pupils use the specific tools to create particular effects and outcomes. By the end of the unit, look for evidence that the children's understanding has developed. Can they cut and paste from different images to create a digital collage? Can they adjust and modify the size, scale and colour of images? Can they use the Layers palette to change the transparency of an image? Do they understand how layers work?

▶ **CD-ROM RESOURCES**
   Presentations: Responding to artists; *Photoshop Elements* Selection tools and layers Masterclass
   Artworks and images
   Resource sheets:
      Layers
      Green screen
      Artist images
   Teacher assessment
   Pupil self-evaluation

SESSION I WORKING WITH LAYERS

LEARNING OBJECTIVES
Children will:

- learn how to use layers and copy and paste between different images to develop creative compositions
- begin to develop an understanding of the potential of layers
- begin to recognise the ways in which layers are used by professional artists.

VOCABULARY **layer, Layer palette, scale, overlay, transparent, visibility, Move tool, cut and paste**

▼ RESOURCES

- ▶ computer
- ▶ image-manipulation software with layers (such as *Photoshop Elements*)
- ▶ printer
- ▶ acetate sheet
- ▶ thick permanent marker pen
- ▶ CD-ROM: Demonstration image I; images of built structures
- ▶ Presentation: *Photoshop Elements* Selection tools and layers Masterclass
- ▶ resource sheet: Layers I

▶ INFORMATION

Saving images: When you create a layered image in *Photoshop* and save it, the extension psd is added to the file name (for example, image I.psd). This is the *Photoshop* default setting and means that all the layers are preserved. If you intend to work on the image again, you must use this format. If the *Photoshop* image is saved as a jpg file, the layers will be lost as this format does not support layers. Only flatten and save as a jpg when the work is complete.

ACTIVITY

In preparation for this session, look at Demonstration image 1 from the CD-ROM. (The Demonstration images can also be viewed in the Presentation: **Photoshop Elements® Selection tools and layers** Masterclass.) Print out the barrage photograph. This session is designed to be used as a stand-alone introduction to layers and should take approximately 20–30 minutes.

- Using an interactive whiteboard, load the barrage photograph from the CD-ROM into the software. On screen, choose the Paintbrush tool and draw a thick line over the image. Explain to the children that if the image were saved and printed, it would become permanent – a photograph with a thick line over it.
- Next place an acetate sheet over the printout of the barrage photograph. Use a marker pen to draw a thick line on the acetate sheet. Explain that the acetate sheet protects the image and can be removed, leaving the image untouched.

- Open another of the built structures images from the CD-ROM using the interactive whiteboard and show pupils how to add a transparent layer to the image. Using the Paint tool, demonstrate how you can now draw lines over the image. In the Layer palette, show them how you can switch the layers on and off to show their visibility.
- Challenge the children to open another image and add a second transparent layer. Ask them to make marks using the Paint tool on the transparent layer. Remind them how to change the visibility of the layers. Question the children about the process and repeat, if needed, to gain a better understanding of the process.

Ask the children to close the image (there is no need to save it).

■ Using the interactive whiteboard, load another of the built structures images on the CD-ROM into the software, and explain that this image will be the background used to overlay other images. Open a second image and demonstrate how to cut a section from this image to overlay onto the first image. Choose the Selection tool and select a portion of the image – it should look as though it has a floating section around it. Then select the Move tool, pick up the section and drag it onto the first image. A second layer is created automatically.

■ Invite pupils to choose any image as their background and challenge them to open a second image, select a section of it and drag it onto their background image. Check they have two images in the Layer palette. Ask them to save the image.

■ Use the interactive whiteboard to show the children how to change the size of their selection by dragging the corner of the image with the Move tool. Click on the dragged selection to fix the new size. In the Layer palette, show the children how to change the transparency of the image by moving the Opacity slider to fade the image into the background.

■ Challenge pupils to scale their image in the same way and to experiment with the Transparency slider. Ask them to save the image.

■ Repeat by opening another image and

practising the process of selecting and dragging the chosen section onto the background image until they have five images including the background.

▼ ASSESSMENT FOR LEARNING

Can the children:
▶ open an image and create a new transparent layer?
▶ draw on the transparent layer without affecting the background layer?
▶ copy a section from one image and paste it onto another image?
▶ use a range of vocabulary to describe what they are doing?

DIFFERENTIATION

Children who have not progressed as far...
It may be helpful for some children to be carefully paired so they can support each other in understanding and using layers.

Children who have progressed further...
Some children who understand the process of cutting and pasting between images could demonstrate to the class using the interactive whiteboard. It may also be useful to identify a small team to act as troubleshooters to support other children when they have completed their own work.

SESSION 2 DIGITAL COLLAGE

LEARNING OBJECTIVES

Children will:

- learn to identify and select appropriate reference and resource materials when designing by selecting images for a digital collage based on the local environment

- develop their understanding of software tools to compose images
- learn about designing and problem-solving skills by creating a layered image.

VOCABULARY collage, Layer palette, Selection tool, Move tool

▼ RESOURCES

- computer
- image-manipulation software with layers (such as *Photoshop Elements*)
- CD-ROM: Demonstration image 2; images of London; images of children's work 1
- resource sheets: Layers 2–4

▼ ASSESSMENT FOR LEARNING

Can the children:

- use digital tools to cut, drag and scale fragments of images?
- use the Selection tool to choose different-sized cuttings to create their layers?
- describe the process of creating a layered composition?

ACTIVITY

The aim of this session is to reinforce the skills from Session 1 in a more purposeful way, using fragments from several different photographs of the local environment to create a digital collage. In preparation for the session, take photographs around the school or local environment and download them onto the computer network in a shared area that pupils can access.

■ Using the interactive whiteboard, open Demonstration image 2 (see the CD-ROM) and talk about the way the image looks. Point out its structure in the Layer palette. Then demonstrate how the image was made.

■ Open one of your images of the local environment (or one of the London images from the CD-ROM) – this is the background image. Remind pupils about layers by showing them the thumbnail (smaller version) of the image in the Layer palette. Open a second image and use the Selection tool to select a rectangular section of this image. Use the Move tool to move the selection to the background image.

■ Challenge the children to do the same. The Layer palette should show two images. Save the image.

■ Ask pupils to repeat this process, selecting different-sized squares and rectangles from different images to add to their background image, until there are five layers (the background image plus four other layers). Ensure they save regularly.

■ At the end of the session, gather the class together at the interactive whiteboard for a discussion about the activity. You may wish to show the children the **Layers** resource sheet to reinforce the process.

DIFFERENTIATION

Children who have not progressed as far...
Some children may find it useful to work in carefully selected pairs so they can help each other.

Children who have progressed further...
Some children may already be familiar with these processes and be able to use the computer tools creatively to create their own design using layers. It may be helpful to group children with prior knowledge of software so they can support each other in extending their experiments and understanding.

SESSION 3 **EDITING LAYERS**

LEARNING OBJECTIVES
Children will:
- learn to understand and use software tools purposefully to achieve their aims by changing the colour, scale, rotation and opacity of layers
- develop confidence and creativity by experimenting with and using different tools and effects.

VOCABULARY Layer palette, visibility, opacity

ACTIVITY

Before the session, see the **Photoshop Elements® Selection tools and layers** Masterclass to remember the structure of the Layer palette. This activity uses a saved image and is designed to practise choosing and editing layers.

- Open Demonstration image 3 (see CD-ROM) on the whiteboard. Discuss the tools the children used to create their layered image in Session 2. Remind them of the structure of the Layer palette and how to switch off the visibility of the layers.
- Switch off layers 2, 3 and 4. Using the Move tool, click on layer 1 to show the children how to move it to a different position over the background image. Point to the corner of the image and show them how to drag the corner to change its size. Double-click to fix the new size. Now show them how to change the opacity of the layer by clicking on the Opacity slider to fade the image into the background. Again in the Layer palette, click on the box that says 'Normal'. A pop-up window shows different options – demonstrate the effect of using some of these.

- Ask pupils to open their image from Session 2 and switch off all layers except the background and layer 1. Challenge them to change the size of the image on layer 1, to change its opacity and to experiment with the effects in the Normal pop-up window.
- Repeat this process with layers 2 to 5 and ask pupils to save their image. They could compare their results with the images of children's work from the CD-ROM.
- Review the process and repeat as necessary so that pupils become confident with the tools. The **Layers** resource sheets can be used to reinforce the process.

RESOURCES

- computer
- image-manipulation software with layers (such as *Photoshop Elements*)
- CD-ROM: Demonstration image 3; images of children's work 2
- resource sheets: Layers 1–4

ASSESSMENT FOR LEARNING

Can the children:
- select individual layers and change the size, colour and opacity of layers?
- describe the different effects that can be created from the Layer palette?

DIFFERENTIATION

Children who have not progressed as far...
Some children may find it useful to work in carefully selected pairs so they can help each other. Additional support may be needed for children who experience difficulty in selecting and understanding the layer tools.

Children who have progressed further...
Some children may be able to use a more varied vocabulary to describe what they have done and may be more willing to explore different tools. Challenge them to show greater control by asking them to reflect, in their work, some of the effects they have seen in a favourite film.

SESSION 4 **ALIEN INVASION**

LEARNING OBJECTIVES
Children will:

- develop their imagination and ability to generate ideas by using a digital camera to capture images for use in their work
- develop their technical skills and creativity in the use of software by experimenting with scale and colour

- begin to understand how artists combine different images to create dramatic compositions for different purposes.

VOCABULARY edit, green screen, Magic wand, scale, enhance, hue, saturation

▼ RESOURCES

- digital cameras
- computer
- image-manipulation software with layers (such as *Photoshop Elements*)
- CD-ROM:
  Demonstration image 4; images of children's green-screen compositions
- Presentation:
  Photoshop Elements Selection tools and layers Masterclass
- resource sheet:
  Green screen

ACTIVITY

This activity is designed to help pupils understand how to photograph objects and prepare them for future projects. The skills learned here can be applied to other sessions and, after completion, the children will understand the necessity for preparing images for creative compositions.

Prior to the session, ask the children to collect and bring in a number of small figures, such as model dinosaurs, Lego, toy cars or robots. You will also need to create a green screen background (see the **Green screen** resource sheet for advice).

■ Talk to pupils about how film-makers appear to place actors in different locations or on different planets, when in reality they do not leave the studio. Explain that they are going to photograph their own models against a green screen and then edit the photographs using image-manipulation software.

■ Ask the children, working in pairs, to arrange their models one by one in front of the green background that you have set up. Encourage them to take two or three pictures of each object from different angles.

■ Download all the photographs onto the computer network in an accessible shared area.

■ Using the interactive whiteboard, open one of the pupils' photographs. Explain that you are going to remove the green background and re-save the image with a white background. Show how the Magic wand tool selects the area of image that is the same colour. Demonstrate using the Magic wand tool to select the green background, and then press the Delete key to remove it. If any green remains, use the Eraser tool to remove it. Save the image, using a new name, into the shared area for future use.

■ Challenge the children to do the same to each of their images, saving each one under a new name.

■ Show pupils Demonstration image 4 (see the CD-ROM) and talk about the composition. On the whiteboard, open one of the images of the local environment and one of the children's model photographs with the background removed. Cut out the object and place it onto the local environment image. Then choose the Magic wand tool and select the background of the model image. Go to the Select menu and choose the Inverse option. Choose the Move tool and drag the model image onto the background image. Now use the Move tool and change the scale of the model.

■ Give the children time to do the same and then repeat the process using the other prepared images. Their final image will have three or more objects on the background image.

■ Talk to the children about reviewing or editing their images, using the interactive whiteboard. Refer them to the Layer palette and talk about the layers and the pictures that are on each layer. Demonstrate how the children can review the layers (see Session 3) so that they are happy with the scale of the objects on each layer.

■ Use the whiteboard again to show the children how to change the colour of the layers. Select a layer and then go to the Enhance menu – Colour – Hue/Saturation. Show the children how to move the sliders to change the colour of the layer. Repeat for the other layers to achieve the desired effect.

▼ ASSESSMENT FOR LEARNING

Can the children:
▶ select and photograph objects from different viewpoints?
▶ prepare images for use in creative compositions?
▶ describe their own and others' work using specialist vocabulary?

DIFFERENTIATION

Children who have not progressed as far…
To give these children a concrete example, they can organise and alter the order of several sheets of paper containing images. You can also reinforce the theme by describing and suggesting a structure for the image and providing further visual references.

Children who have progressed further…
More confident children may find it helpful to work alongside each other to provide mutual support and opportunities to learn from each other. They should be challenged to develop further control by identifying specific outcomes to work towards, rather than simply accepting random effects defined by the software.

SESSION 5 FANTASTIC ENVIRONMENTS

LEARNING OBJECTIVES
Children will:

- develop creativity and imagination by applying what they have learned to create an expressive fantasy image
- extend and consolidate their understanding of tools and processes by working with increasing independence
- develop the capacity to prepare, plan and design
- extend their knowledge and understanding of art and artists by learning about artists who created fantasy images.

VOCABULARY **transform, exotic, exaggerate, review, visibility, scale**

▼ **RESOURCES**

- ▸ computer
- ▸ image-manipulation software with layers (such as *Photoshop Elements*)
- ▸ images of the school environment and exotic fruit or flowers
- ▸ CD-ROM: Demonstration image 5; images of exotic fruit fruit
- ▸ Presentation: Responding to artists
- ▸ resource sheets: Green screen; Artist images
- ▸ pupil self-evaluation sheet

ACTIVITY

This activity builds on the skills used in Sessions 3 and 4 and encourages the children to create a fantastic environment, using exotic plants to transform a photograph of the school environment. In preparation for this activity, take two sets of photographs – one of the school environment and another of exotic fruit and flowers (or use the images on the CD-ROM) – and download them all into the shared area on the computer. If practical, pupils could take their own photographs of exotic fruit and flowers. Use the green screen method described in Session 4 for photographing objects (see also the **Green screen** resource sheet). The session may take longer than one lesson as pupils may want to

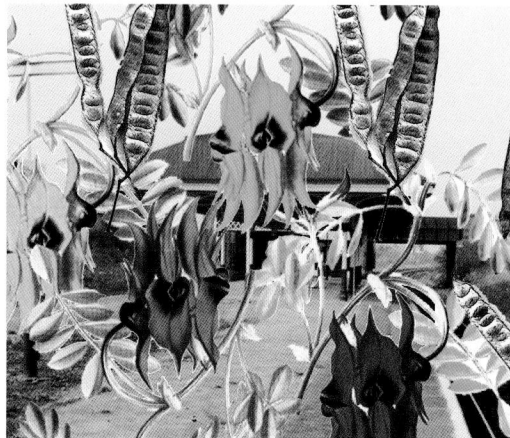

go off on a tangent, explore, draft and redraft their plans.

■ Talk to the children about the work of Max Ernst and Henri Rousseau, and show contemporary images from film and animation (see the **Artist images** resource sheet). Display the works on the interactive whiteboard. Ask pupils to describe the images and discuss the composition of the works. (Refer to the **Responding to artists** Presentation on the CD-ROM.)

■ Ask the children to use printouts to make a drawing to plan their composition before starting work on the computer. Using squared/grid paper may be a help to some pupils. Encourage them to exaggerate the scale of the fruit and flowers to create a dramatic composition.

■ On the interactive whiteboard, show a slideshow of the images from the school environment and the images of exotic fruit and flowers. Explain to the children that they are going to

choose one image from the school environment as a background and turn it into a fantastic environment by adding the exotic fruit and flowers.

■ Open the school environment image and one of the pictures of the exotic fruit (see Demonstration image 5 on the CD-ROM). Demonstrate how to cut the fruit from the page using the Magic wand and then inverse the selection. Use the Move tool to drag the fruit to the background image.

■ Challenge the children to do the same, using their plans as a guide, and repeat the process using different fruit or flowers until they have five layers, including the background.

■ Gather pupils together to review the layers. Remind them how to change the visibility of the layers. Talk about the scale of the fruit and where it could be positioned. Objects that are in the foreground of the image will be larger than the ones in the background. Switch on the next layer and scale this up or down to suit the composition.

■ Ask the children to review their layers, looking at each one in turn. Remind them that they can change the transparency of the layer by experimenting with the Opacity slider. Save the image.

■ Show pupils how to change the colour of the layers on the whiteboard. Select a layer and then go to the Enhance menu – Colour – Hue/Saturation. Show them how to move the sliders to change the colour of the layer. Repeat the process, changing the colour of each layer. Save the resulting image.

■ At the end of the session, provide each child with a **Pupil self-evaluation** sheet for feedback on the work undertaken in the unit.

▼ ASSESSMENT FOR LEARNING

Can the children:
▸ create an original fantasy digital collage using images from different sources?
▸ use the software to follow through or deliberately adapt their original designs?
▸ use software with confidence and resolve problems independently?
▸ talk about the qualities in their own and others' work and express preferences?

DIFFERENTIATION

Children who have not progressed as far…
Reinforce the theme with these children by talking further about the artists' fantastic landscapes and the ways that forms can be exaggerated. More adult support in explaining and demonstrating the software processes may be helpful, as would judicious grouping.

Children who have progressed further…
Children who have more confidence in using the software can experiment further by adding extra layers and experimenting with the filters and other effects. They could use the interactive whiteboard to demonstrate to others what they have learned.

OTHER AREAS OF LEARNING

LITERACY

■ Ask pupils to write a short poem or story to describe an alien invasion of the school or local area.

■ The children can look for examples and talk about the ways in which digital media and image manipulation are used on television and in film. Do photographs lie?

■ Use a multi-layered image relating to a narrative poem as a starting point for class discussion.

GEOGRAPHY

■ Relate to the topic 'Investigating our local area'. Pupils can explore the local area and use ICT to imagine how it might have looked 100 years ago and how it might look 100 years into the future.

Digital media

ART AND DESIGN

■ Challenge the children to look at the work of different sculptors and design their own imaginative sculpture for the local environment.

SCIENCE

■ Pupils can use a range of materials to create a model of a toy or puppet that has moving parts.

PHYSICAL, SOCIAL AND HEALTH EDUCATION (PSHE)

■ Create opportunities for pupils to work together at the computer, to share ideas and problem-solve in pairs and groups.

■ Engage the children in a discussion about living in different environments and communities.